Global Hegemony
A Strategic Illusion

NATO Expansion, Nuclear
Promises & the Death of Strategic
Trust

Bahaa G. Arnouk

ISBN: 978-1-0683791-3-0

Book Cover by Bahaa G. Arnouk

1st edition 2025

Table of Contents

Introduction

In the pale light of a snow-blanketed February morning in 1990, inside the austere corridors of the Kremlin, a quiet but historic conversation took place. U.S. Secretary of State James Baker leaned across a polished table and assured Mikhail Gorbachev—then the leader of a crumbling Soviet Union—that NATO would not expand "one inch eastward." Gorbachev, weary but hopeful, nodded. In that moment, between fading empires and trembling ideologies, trust flickered like a candle in the wind.

This book begins there—with a promise. A promise made not in fanfare, but in fragile sincerity. A promise that would echo through decades of strategic miscalculations, broken assurances, and geopolitical pivots that reshaped the fate of nations.

Global Hegemony: A Strategic Illusion is not merely a chronicle of military alliances or diplomatic treaties. It is a journey through the labyrinth of post-Cold War history, a guided unravelling of the seductive myth that dominance equals stability, that might ensure right, and that the world can be reordered by the few, for the many, without consequence.

I, invite you to step beyond the headlines and policy papers, and into the rooms where real history was written—in private memos, in whispered negotiations, in the unsaid tensions between words. What you will discover is a different kind of narrative, one in which the world's most powerful nations played a high-stakes game with the very essence of global trust.

After the Cold War, when the Iron Curtain fell and statues of Lenin toppled like dominoes across Eastern Europe, a rare window opened—a moment when history could have bent toward reconciliation. The Warsaw Pact dissolved, the Soviet Union collapsed, and for a fleeting instant, it seemed the old world order might give way to something nobler: a shared European home, built not on rivalry, but respect.

But promises, like empires, are delicate things.

In this book, you will read of how that moment was lost— not all at once, but piece by piece. You'll witness how NATO, once a twelve-member Atlantic defence pact, quietly expanded its borders across lands once promised neutrality. From the forests of Poland to the Black Sea shores of Bulgaria, from the Baltic republics to the gates of Ukraine, the alliance advanced, often under the banner of peace, but perceived—rightfully or not—as a creeping wall of containment.

You'll trace how arms control treaties, once the backbone of Cold War deterrence, began to fray. The logic of MAD—Mutually Assured Destruction—gave way to a less stable, more dangerous ambiguity, as old agreements like INF and START were abandoned or hollowed out. Nuclear silos once silenced were eyed again with suspicion. Inspection teams were replaced by rhetoric. Dialogue gave way to doctrine.

You'll also hear the voices of those who warned us—diplomats, presidents, military officers—who spoke of red lines and strategic restraint, only to be drowned out by the drumbeat of expansion and exceptionalism.

But this is not just a book of the past. It is a mirror held to the present. Because the illusion persists.

The illusion that one bloc, one system, one alliance can dictate the terms of global order indefinitely without generating friction, resistance, or blowback. The illusion that trust can be bent without breaking. That global security is a zero-sum game where more weapons, more members, and more promises made to some—but broken to others—can somehow lead to peace.

As I, explore in these pages, the real battleground is not merely geography—it is psychology. Strategic illusions are powerful because they feel safe. But in reality, they are fault lines waiting to rupture.

We live today in a world once again shadowed by confrontation. The dream of a "Common European Home" has faded into contested borders and sanctioned economies. The logic of collective security has been replaced by spheres of influence and renewed arms races.

And still, the architects of hegemony insist it was all inevitable. That the expansion of power always leads to stability.

But history—if we are brave enough to read it honestly—says otherwise.

This book is an appeal to that honesty. It is a call to remember the promises made, to re-examine the choices taken, and to understand that true strategic strength lies not in illusions of dominance, but in the clarity of trust, the humility of restraint, and the courage to imagine a different path.

Let us begin.

Chapter (1)

"Not One Inch Eastward": The Broken Pledge That Shaped Europe

"There would be no extension of NATO's jurisdiction for forces of NATO one inch to the east"

U.S. Secretary of State James Baker

The **North Atlantic Treaty Organization (NATO)** was established on 4th April 1949, as a collective defence alliance among twelve founding nations: the United States, Canada, the United Kingdom, France, Belgium, the Netherlands, Luxembourg, Norway, Denmark, Italy, Portugal, and Iceland. The primary purpose of NATO was to provide mutual defense against aggression, particularly in response to the growing influence of the Soviet Union in Europe during the early stages of the Cold War.

NATO's foundational aim was to ensure the security and freedom of its member countries through political and military means. The alliance was built on the principle that an armed attack against one or more of its members would be considered an attack against them all, as outlined in Article 5 of the North Atlantic Treaty.

President Harry S. Truman played a pivotal role in the formation of NATO and articulated its significance during the signing ceremony. In his address on 4th April 1949, President Truman emphasized the treaty's defensive nature and its role in promoting peace:

"In this pact, we hope to create a shield against aggression and the fear of aggression—a bulwark which will permit us to get on with the real business of government and society, the business of achieving a fuller and happier life for all our citizens[1]."

He further underscored the treaty's intent to prevent war:

"The essential purpose of the North Atlantic Treaty is to prevent war through the creation of conditions under which resort to war is clearly unattractive to any potential aggressor.[2]"

President Truman also highlighted the proactive steps taken to maintain peace:

---

[1] Rare Chance to View Original NATO Treaty | National Archives - https://www.archives.gov/press/press-releases/2019/nr19-42?

[2] 20161130_19490404__Opening_address_Truman-s.pdf - https://www.nato.int/nato_static_fl2014/assets/pdf/history_pdf/20161130_19490404__Opening_address_Truman-s.pdf?

"Even without that agreement, which we still hope for, we shall do as much as we can. And every bit that we do will add to the strength of the fabric of peace throughout the world[3]."

These statements reflect the U.S. leadership's commitment to establishing NATO as a means of collective security, aiming to deter aggression and promote stability in the North Atlantic region.

NATO First Expansion: From 12 to 16

1952 – Greece and Turkey Join

In response to the Soviet threat in the Mediterranean and Middle East, **Greece and Turkey** were admitted into NATO. Their inclusion extended NATO's strategic depth and placed pressure on the USSR's southern flank.

1955 – West Germany Joins

Perhaps the most controversial expansion at the time, **West Germany** became NATO's 15th member. This marked a key turning point, symbolizing the reintegration of West Germany into the Western defense structure. In direct response, the Soviet Union formed the Warsaw Pact just days later, consolidating its Eastern Bloc allies under a military alliance.

1982 – Spain Joins

---

[3] Address on the Occasion of the Signing of the North Atlantic Treaty | The American Presidency Project - https://www.presidency.ucsb.edu/documents/address-the-occasion-the-signing-the-north-atlantic-treaty?

Following the end of Franco's dictatorship and its transition to democracy, Spain became the 16th NATO member in May 1982. Spain brought NATO access to key geostrategic locations such as the Mediterranean and Strait of Gibraltar.

Cold War Role and Strategic Evolution (1950s–1990)

NATO's development during the Cold War went beyond just expanding membership. The alliance underwent significant strategic and political transformation:

Massive Retaliation to Flexible Response

NATO's 1950s "Massive Retaliation" doctrine promised overwhelming nuclear response to any Soviet aggression (inspired by U.S. Secretary of State John Foster Dulles). Additionally, NATO adopted in the 1967 MC 14/3 "Flexible Response" strategy, allowing a graduated response to conflict — starting with conventional arms and escalating only if necessary.

Nuclear Sharing and U.S. Umbrella

The U.S. deployed thousands of tactical nuclear weapons across Europe as part of NATO deterrence. Host countries included: West Germany, Belgium, the Netherlands, Italy, Turkey, and others. These were deployed under the Nuclear Sharing framework where non-nuclear NATO members hosted U.S. weapons with joint decision-making protocols.

Political Integration and Crises

In 1966, France withdrew from NATO's integrated military command under Charles de Gaulle, although it remained a political member. NATO had to relocate its headquarters from Paris to Brussels, where it remains today. France fully returned to NATO's command structure in 2009.

Détente and Dual-Track Policy (1970s–80s)

NATO supported arms control talks like SALT I (1972) and the Helsinki Accords (1975). In 1979, NATO adopted the dual-track decision:

- Deploy U.S. Pershing II and cruise missiles to counter Soviet SS-20s.

- Simultaneously pursue arms control negotiations with the USSR.

This led to large-scale anti-nuclear protests, particularly in West Germany, the UK, and the Netherlands.

The Rise and Fall of the Warsaw Pact: Echoes from Soviet Leadership

By the mid-1950s, the geopolitical landscape of Europe was shifting rapidly. The integration of West Germany into NATO on May 9, 1955, was perceived by the Soviet Union as a direct threat to its sphere of influence. In response, on 14th May 1955, the Soviet Union and seven Eastern European nations convened in Warsaw to establish a counterbalancing alliance: the Warsaw Pact. This treaty, officially named the *Treaty of Friendship, Cooperation, and Mutual Assistance*, aimed to solidify mutual defence commitments among its members.

Nikita Khrushchev, the First Secretary of the Communist Party of the Soviet Union, later reflected on this period, believing that after creating the Warsaw Pact, the time had come to think about a reduction of armed forces.

The Eastern Bloc's Unified Front

The founding members of the Warsaw Pact were Soviet Union, Albania (withdrew in 1968), Bulgaria, Czechoslovakia, East Germany (departed in 1990 prior to German reunification), Hungary, Poland and Romania.

This coalition was not merely a military alliance but also a mechanism for the Soviet Union to maintain control over its satellite states, ensuring alignment with its policies and suppressing any deviations.

Internal Struggles and Suppressed Aspirations

The Warsaw Pact's primary purpose was collective defence against external aggression. However, it also served as an instrument for the Soviet Union to intervene in member states' affairs. Notably, in 1956, when Hungary attempted to break free from Soviet influence and withdraw from the Pact, Soviet forces invaded to quash the revolution. Similarly, the 1968 Prague Spring in Czechoslovakia was met with a swift military response to halt liberal reforms.

The Dissolution of the Pact

The late 1980s ushered in winds of change across Eastern Europe. Mikhail Gorbachev's policies of *perestroika* (restructuring) and *glasnost* (openness) led to increased political freedoms and a re-evaluation of Soviet relationships with its neighbours. Gorbachev emphasized the importance of political solutions over military interventions, stating, *"The leaders of our two countries cannot act as fire brigades[4]."*

As democratic movements gained momentum, member states began asserting their independence. Recognizing the shifting tides, Gorbachev speaking to the UN in the general assembly on December 7, 1988:

"Today I can inform you of the following: The Soviet Union has made a decision on reducing its armed forces. In the next two years,

---

[4] Malta summit ends the cold war – archive, 1989 | Europe | The Guardian -
Https://www.theguardian.com/world/2024/nov/27/malta-summit-ends-the-cold-war-archive-1989?

their numerical strength will be reduced by 500,000 persons, and the volume of conventional arms will also be cut considerably. These reductions will be made on a unilateral basis, unconnected with negotiations on the mandate for the Vienna meeting. By agreement with our allies in the Warsaw Pact, we have made the decision to withdraw six tank divisions from the GDR, Czechoslovakia, and Hungary, and to disband them by 1991[5]".

These developments culminated in the formal dissolution of the Warsaw Pact on July 1, 1991, symbolizing the end of an era and the redefinition of European alliances.

Echoes of a Promise: The Quiet Betrayal of Gorbachev

In the frozen heart of February 1990, as the Cold War began its slow and uncertain thaw, U.S. Secretary of State James Baker sat across from Soviet leader Mikhail Gorbachev in the austere Kremlin. A pivotal question trembled in the air between them: What would become of NATO if Germany reunified?

With Germany's future hanging in the balance and the Soviet Union teetering at the edge of economic and political collapse, **Baker** made a now-famous assurance to Mikhail Gorbachev in Moscow on 9 February 1990 not

---

[5] Excerpts of Address by Mikhail Gorbachev. 43rd U.N. General Assembly Session, December 7, 1988 - Excerpts of Address by Mikhail Gorbachev. 43rd U.N. General Assembly Session, December 7, 1988

once, but three separate times that NATO forces won't move on inch to the east:

"We understand the need for assurances to the countries in the East. If we maintain a presence in a Germany that is a part of NATO, there would be no extension of NATO's jurisdiction for forces of NATO one inch to the east[6]."

He even posed the question to Gorbachev:

"Would you prefer a united Germany outside of NATO that is independent and has no U.S. forces, or a united Germany in NATO with assurances that NATO's jurisdiction would not move eastward?

To Gorbachev, this wasn't mere diplomacy. It was a commitment—one repeated by Baker multiple times that day, including to Soviet Foreign Minister Eduard Shevardnadze, and the next day on 10 February 1990 affirmed by Chancellor Helmut Kohl during his meeting in Moscow with Gorbachev:

"We believe that NATO should not expand the sphere of its activity. We have to find a reasonable resolution. I correctly understand the security interests of the Soviet Union, and I realize

---

[6] U.S. Department of State, FOIA 199504567 (National Security Archive Flashpoints Collection, Box 38) - https://nsarchive.gwu.edu/briefing-book/russia-programs/2017-12-12/nato-expansion-what-gorbachev-heard-western-leaders-early

that you, Mr. General Secretary, and the Soviet leadership will have to clearly explain what is happening to the Soviet people[7]".

The Chorus of Promises

In the months that followed, a string of Western leaders—representing the United States, the United Kingdom, France, and Germany—voiced similar assurances. Some were captured in confidential cables, others in transcripts, and still others recalled by aides and ministers present at the meetings.

German Foreign Minister Hans-Dietrich Genscher, in his landmark *Tutzing speech* on 31 January 1990, was unequivocal:

"That the changes in Eastern Europe and the German unification process must not lead to an 'impairment of Soviet security interests.' Therefore, NATO should rule out an 'expansion of its territory towards the east, i.e. moving it closer to the Soviet borders[8]."

Douglas Hurd, the British Foreign Secretary, echoed this to Genscher:

"When he talked about not wanting to extend NATO that applied to other states beside the GDR. The Russians must have some

---

[7] Memorandum of conversation between Mikhail Gorbachev and Helmut Kohl - Mikhail Gorbachev i germanskii vopros, edited by Alexander Galkin and Anatoly Chernyaev, (Moscow: Ves Mir, 2006) - https://nsarchive.gwu.edu/briefing-book/russia-programs/2017-12-12/nato-expansion-what-gorbachev-heard-western-leaders-early

[8] U.S. Embassy Bonn Confidential Cable to Secretary of State on the speech of the German Foreign Minister: Genscher Outlines His Vision of a New European Architecture.- U.S. Department of State. FOIA Reading Room. Case F-2015 10829

assurance that if, for example, the Polish Government left the Warsaw Pact one day, they would not join NATO the next.[9]"

British Prime Minister John Major, in a face-to-face with Soviet military officers, responded directly to Marshal Dmitry Yazov:

"We are not talking about strengthening of NATO... I do not foresee circumstances now or in the future where East European countries would become members of NATO[10]."

French President François Mitterrand in a record of a conversation with Mikhail Gorbachev on 25 May 1990 says:

"I always told my NATO partners: make a commitment not to move NATO's military formations from their current territory in the FRG to East Germany"[11].

Margaret Thatcher, known for her hawkish stance, agreed in 8 June 1990 during a visit to Gorbachev to: *"find ways to give the Soviet Union confidence that its security would be assured.[12]"*

---

[9] Mr. Hurd to Sir C. Mallaby (Bonn). Telegraphic N. 85: Secretary of State's Call on Herr Genscher: German Unification.- Documents on British Policy Overseas, series III, volume VII: German Unification, 1989-1990. (Foreign and Commonwealth Office. Documents on British Policy Overseas, edited by Patrick Salmon, Keith Hamilton, and Stephen Twigge, Oxford and New York, Routledge 2010). pp. 261-264 -

[10] Ambassador Rodric Braithwaite diary, 05 March 1991-
https://nsarchive.gwu.edu/briefing-book/russia-programs/2017-12-12/nato-expansion-what-gorbachev-heard-western-leaders-early

[11] Record of conversation between Mikhail Gorbachev and Francois Mitterrand (excerpts) - Mikhail Gorbachev i germanskii vopros, edited by Alexander Galkin and Anatoly Chernyaev, (Moscow: Ves Mir, 2006), pp. 454-466

[12] Letter from Mr. Powell (N. 10) to Mr. Wall: Thatcher-Gorbachev memorandum of conversation - Documents on British Policy Overseas, series III, volume VII: German Unification, 1989-1990. (Foreign and Commonwealth Office. Documents on British Policy

Gorbachev emphasized the need for NATO and the Warsaw pact to move closer together, from confrontation to cooperation to build a new Europe: *"We must mould European structures so that they helped us find the common European home. Neither side must be afraid of unorthodox solutions[13]"*

There was a consensus—spoken, if not signed. In exchange for the Soviet Union's acceptance of a united Germany in NATO, the West would not advance the alliance into Eastern Europe. These were not side comments or informal musings—they were the backbone of the conversations shaping post-Cold War Europe.

Yet, no legally binding treaty emerged. And while the ink dried on the Treaty on the Final Settlement with Respect to Germany (Sept 1990), the spirit of those early 1990 promises began to evaporate.

"The West is outplaying us, promising to respect the interests of the USSR, but in practice, step by step, separating us from 'traditional Europe.[14]*"* - **Valentin Falin memo to Gorbachev, April 1990.**

Overseas, edited by Patrick Salmon, Keith Hamilton, and Stephen Twigge, Oxford and New York, Routledge 2010), pp 411-417

[13] Letter from Mr. Powell (N. 10) to Mr. Wall: Thatcher-Gorbachev memorandum of conversation - Documents on British Policy Overseas, series III, volume VII: German Unification, 1989-1990. (Foreign and Commonwealth Office. Documents on British Policy Overseas, edited by Patrick Salmon, Keith Hamilton, and Stephen Twigge, Oxford and New York, Routledge 2010), pp 411-417

[14] Valentin Falin Memorandum to Mikhail Gorbachev (Excerpts) - Mikhail Gorbachev i germanskii vopros, edited by Alexander Galkin and Anatoly Chernyaev, (Moscow: Ves Mir, 2006), pp. 398-408

The West had already begun building a new strategic reality - one far different than what Gorbachev had been led to believe.

While Gorbachev envisioned a *"Common European Home,"* Washington and Brussels were beginning to quietly pivot. Internal memos from the U.S. State Department (Oct 1990) indicate that discussions about NATO's future role—including potential East European membership— had already begun.

The NATO That Grew

In a visit of Boris Yeltsin from Russian Supreme Soviet Delegation to NATO HQ in Brussels on 1st July 1991, and during a meeting with the NATO leadership, additional assurances were given to the Russians from the highest levels of NATO – Secretary General Manfred Woerner who assured that NATO expansion is not happening:

"The principal task of the next decade will be to build a new European security structure, to include the Soviet Union and the Warsaw Pact nation... We should not allow the isolation of the USSR from the European community"[15].

With the ink still drying on the "Two Plus Four" Treaty of 1990 (which included assurances about the special military status of East Germany), the Warsaw Pact disbanded in 1991. The Soviet Union itself collapsed

[15] Memorandum to Boris Yeltsin from Russian Supreme Soviet delegation to NATO HQs - State Archive of the Russian Federation (GARF), Fond 10026, Opis 1

months later. Suddenly, the very architecture that Gorbachev thought would guarantee equilibrium no longer existed.

On 31st January 1994, U.S. President Bill Clinton, speaking at NATO Headquarters in Brussels, launched the **Partnership for Peace (PfP)** — a strategic initiative to bring former Eastern Bloc countries into closer cooperation with NATO.

Speaking to an invited audience of university professors, ethnic leaders, businessmen, and grammar school students in Fisher Hall in 22 October 1996, the president described the United States in the post Cold War era as *"the indispensable nation."*

The president warned that the NATO expansion plan: *"is not free of cost. Peace and security cannot be had on the cheap. And enlargement will mean extending the most solemn security guarantee to our new Allies a commitment to treat an attack on one as an attack on all. But mark my words, if we fail to seize this historic opportunity to build a new NATO in a new Europe, if we allow the Iron Curtain to be replaced by a veil of indifference, we will pay a much higher price later on down the road[16]"*

The Russian President Boris Yeltsin warned that full NATO expansion would be a betrayal of earlier

---

[16] NATO Speech by Pres. Clinton - 22 Oct. 1996 -
https://www.nato.int/docu/speech/1996/s961022a.htm#:~:text=But%20mark%20my%20words%2C%20if,later%20on%20down%20the%20road.

understandings. His letter to Clinton in 15th September 1993 stated:

"I also want to call attention to the fact that the spirit of the treaty on the final settlement with respect to Germany, signed in September 1990, especially its provisions that prohibit the development of foreign troops within the eastern lands of the Federal Republic of Germany, precludes the option of expanding the NATO zone into the East[17]"

Also on 3rd December 1994, Yelstin again in a letter to US president Bill Clinton say:

"But we need assurances that enlargement. Rather than partnership, is not being emphasized now. The problem should be tackled as a large-scale one. there should be dialogue on adopting specific obligations and security guarantees for Russia and NATO which would correspond to the nature of radical changes in the European situation.[18]"

Still, the process began — cautiously at first, then with unstoppable momentum.

[17] Retranslation of Yeltsin letter on NATO expansion | National Security Archive - https://nsarchive.gwu.edu/document/16376-document-04-retranslation-yeltsin-letter
[18] Yeltsin Letter to Clinton | National Security Archive - https://nsarchive.gwu.edu/document/27163-doc-09-yeltsin-letter-clinton

Waves of NATO Expansion

From 1999 to 2024, NATO expanded from 16 to 32 members, with each new wave moving the alliance closer to Russia's borders.

1999 – Poland, Hungary, Czech Republic

On **12 March 1999**, NATO welcomed its first three post-Warsaw Pact members: **Poland, Hungary, and the Czech Republic**.

This milestone coincided with NATO's 50th anniversary and came during the Kosovo conflict, deepening Russian suspicion. *"Our commitment to enlargement is part of a broader strategy of projecting stability and working together with our Partners to build a Europe whole and free[19]."*

Moscow called the move a violation of the post-Cold War security consensus.

2004 – "The Big Bang": 7 Nations Join

In March 2004, NATO admitted seven nations: Estonia, Latvia, Lithuania, Slovakia, Slovenia, Romania, and Bulgaria — the largest single expansion to date. President George W. Bush emphasized that NATO's enlargement aimed to promote European unity and security, not to threaten Russia. He stated:

---

[19] NATO Press Release NAC-S(99)64 - 24 April 1999 - https://www.nato.int/docu/pr/1999/p99-064e.htm?

"The NATO alliance now flies seven new flags, and reaches from the Bay of Biscay to the Black Sea. And Europe - once the source of global conflict - is now a force for stability and peace[20]."

For Russia, this was deeply provocative, especially the inclusion of the Baltic states, once Soviet republics. Putin strongly objected the expansion of NATO. In a meeting with NATO leaders on the side of NATO Bucharest Summit 4th April 2008, he stressed the NATO leaders to listen to Russia's concerns over NATO's plans to admit Ukraine and Georgia in the future, saying:

"The emergence of the powerful military bloc at our borders will be seen as a direct threat to Russia's security... I heard them saying today that the expansion is not directed against Russia. But it's the potential, not intentions, that matter... We want to be heard, and we want to see problems that divide us solved.[21]"

2009 – Albania and Croatia

In April 2009, Albania and Croatia joined NATO during the Strasbourg-Kehl summit. Though less controversial

---

[20] NATO - Opinion: Remarks by US President George W. Bush at the NATO Accession Ceremony in Washington D.C., USA, 29-Mar.-2004 -
https://www.nato.int/cps/en/natohq/opinions_21295.htm?selectedLocale=en
[21] Stay away, Vladimir Putin tells Nato —
https://www.telegraph.co.uk/news/worldnews/1584027/Stay-away-Vladimir-Putin-tells-Nato.html?msockid=105a39b5d5fb67fd2ca52c9bd440663a&ICID=continue_without_subscribing_reg_first

than earlier enlargements, it continued to extend NATO's presence in the Balkans.

2017 – Montenegro

Despite internal opposition and a Russian-backed coup attempt, Montenegro became NATO's 29th member on 5th June 2017. This accession was met with strong opposition from Russia, which viewed it as a threat to regional stability. The Russian Foreign Ministry issued a statement on the day of Montenegro's accession, stating:

"In the light of the hostile course chosen by the Montenegrin authorities, the Russian side reserves the right to take retaliatory measures on a reciprocal basis. In politics, just as in physics, for every action there is an opposite reaction[22]."

2020 – North Macedonia

North Macedonia joined NATO on 27th March 2020, following a protracted name dispute resolution with Greece. Upon North Macedonia's accession, NATO Secretary General Jens Stoltenberg remarked:

"North Macedonia is now part of the NATO family, a family of 30 nations and almost one billion people. A family based on the

---

[22] Russia threatens retaliation as Montenegro becomes 29th NATO member | Reuters - https://www.reuters.com/article/us-usa-nato-montenegro-idUSKBN18W2WS/

certainty that, no matter what challenges we face, we are all stronger and safer together."

The U.S. Department of State also issued a statement emphasizing the significance of this development:

"North Macedonia's NATO membership will support greater integration, democratic reform, trade, security, and stability across the region[23]."

Russia expressed discontent regarding North Macedonia's NATO membership. In 2019, prior to the accession, Russian President Vladimir Putin accused the West of destabilizing the Balkans by encouraging countries like North Macedonia to join NATO.

Furthermore, the Russian Ministry of Foreign Affairs issued a critical statement following North Macedonia's accession, suggesting that the country's inclusion in NATO was of little consequence to the alliance's military and political potential.

2023 – Finland

In a watershed moment driven by Russia's 2022 invasion of Ukraine, Finland abandoned its neutrality and formally joined NATO on 4th April 2023. NATO Secretary General Jens Stoltenberg acknowledged the strategic impact of Finland's membership. In a joint press

---

[23] North Macedonia Joins the NATO Alliance - United States Department of State - https://2017-2021.state.gov/north-macedonia-joins-the-nato-alliance/?

conference with Finnish President Sauli Niinistö on 4th April 2023, he stated:

"By becoming a member, Finland is now covered by the security guarantees enshrined in Article 5 of the North Atlantic Treaty. NATO stands with Finland."

Russia's reaction, officials expressed intentions to implement countermeasures in response to NATO's expansion. This indicates Russia's perception of Finland's NATO membership as a security concern, leading to plans for military adjustments along its border.

2024 – Sweden

Sweden officially became the 32nd member of NATO on 7th March 2024, after over two centuries of military non-alignment. Sweden's accession followed the delayed ratifications by Turkey and Hungary. Turkey approved Sweden's NATO membership in late January 2024, and Hungary's parliament ratified the accession protocol on 26 February 2024.

Upon Sweden's accession, NATO Secretary General Jens Stoltenberg stated:

"This is a historic day. Sweden will now take its rightful place at NATO's table, with an equal say in shaping NATO policies and decisions. After over 200 years of non-alignment, Sweden now enjoys the protection granted under Article 5, the ultimate guarantee of Allies' freedom and security. Sweden brings with it capable armed

forces and a first-class defence industry. Sweden's accession makes NATO stronger, Sweden safer, and the whole Alliance more secure[24].

From 16 to 32: The Expanding Arc

When the Cold War ended, NATO had 16 members. By 2024, it had 32 — including 14 countries that were once part of the Warsaw Pact or the USSR. This expansion formed a strategic arc around Russia's western frontier — from the Baltic to the Black Sea. To Moscow, this **wasn't integration**. It was **encirclement**.

Lavrov criticized NATO's expansion, stating that such actions would undermine prospects for dialogue on European security[25]:

"NATO's reckless expansion eastwards, northwards or to other geographical areas undermines the very prospects to continue normal communication on European security…unfortunately, we are witnessing this process amid NATO's absorption of almost all neutral nations…that's sad" …. *"When and if the West comes to its senses and realizes that it will not be able to reverse the historically unbiased process of a multipolar world order evolving, that will, of*

[24] NATO - News: Sweden officially joins NATO , 07-Mar.-2024 - https://www.nato.int/cps/en/natohq/news_223446.htm?
[25] Russian news agency - NATO's 'reckless' expansion to undermine chances for security dialogue — Lavrov - Russian Politics & Diplomacy - TASS - https://tass.com/politics/1618823?fbclid=IwAR3E48ZS4zmHFHrUERipqQ-sb9xa2r9sIbmvp4Fc7UGhXV8unrR1FCc-Psk%2Famp&utm_source

course, require a conversation that will not be limited to Europe only."

Chapter Conclusion: A Promise in the Snow, a Shadow on the Horizon

In the pale light of February 1990, when the world still trembled from the Cold War's long chill, promises were whispered across mahogany tables and cold Kremlin corridors. "Not one inch eastward," said the Americans. "We understand your security concerns," echoed the Germans. "NATO is not a threat," assured the British and the French. And in that fragile moment—amid collapsing empires and swelling hopes—Mikhail Gorbachev chose trust over fear.

But history, as it often does, took another route.

From twelve founding members encircling the Atlantic to thirty-two stretching deep into Eastern Europe, NATO's arc now reaches from the Arctic Circle to the Black Sea. The alliance has grown not just in numbers, but in mission, geography, and controversy. And what began as a defensive pact against a Cold War foe evolved—deliberately or not—into the very thing it once claimed it would never become: a presence on Russia's doorstep.

For Moscow, this wasn't just a geopolitical development—it was a psychological break, a post-Soviet humiliation. Each new flag added to NATO's banner pulled a memory thread from a time when the USSR once stood shoulder to shoulder with the West to defeat fascism—only to later be promised cooperation and delivered containment.

Yet amidst this growing divide, there were moments— brief, luminous—when both sides reached for something greater: arms control. Treaties were signed. Warheads were dismantled. Silos stood empty. From the **Limited Test Ban Treaty** to **START I**, from **INF** to **SORT**, and even **Open Skies**, diplomats and generals alike dared to believe that stability could be negotiated—even when trust could not.

But as NATO expanded eastward, many of those agreements began to fray—or fall. Some were violated, others abandoned, a few torn apart by shifting leadership and hardening rhetoric. What began as cooperative disarmament turned into mutual disengagement.

And so the story of post-Cold War Europe isn't just about borders and blocs. It's about the **balance between promise and power**, and how that balance shaped everything from missile silos in Siberia to radar domes in Poland.

The next chapters turn the gaze to that delicate dance— to the language of red lines, inspection teams, countdown clocks, and codes never meant to be used. A world where the weight of survival rested not in tanks or treaties alone, but in trust. Or the loss of it.

Chapter (2)

The International Atomic Energy Agency (IAEA) – A Guardian of Nuclear Peace and Progress

"This greatest of destructive forces can be developed into a great boon, for the benefit of all mankind"

Dwight D. Eisenhower (U.S. President)

The Historical Genesis: A World at the Nuclear Crossroads

The mid-20th century was a period of unparalleled scientific advancement and geopolitical turmoil. The detonation of atomic bombs over **Hiroshima and Nagasaki in 1945** demonstrated the terrifying destructive power of nuclear energy. It was a watershed moment that reshaped global politics, prompting nations to grapple with an urgent question: Could nuclear technology be harnessed for progress rather than destruction?

The world had entered the **atomic age**, and with it came an era of anxiety, rivalry, and ambition. The **United States** and the **Soviet Union** emerged as the two dominant superpowers, racing to expand their nuclear arsenals while the rest of the world sought assurances that atomic energy would not lead to catastrophe.

Amid this uncertainty, a vision for a new global institution took shape. In **1953**, U.S. President **Dwight D. Eisenhower** delivered his landmark **Atoms for Peace** speech at the United Nations General Assembly, calling for an international agency to promote the peaceful use of nuclear energy:

"The United States knows that peaceful power from atomic energy is no dream of the future. That capability, already proved, is here— now—today... This greatest of destructive forces can be developed into a great boon, for the benefit of all mankind."

Eisenhower's speech ignited diplomatic discussions, and after extensive negotiations, the **International Atomic Energy Agency (IAEA)** was formally established on July 29, 1957, following the adoption of its Statute on October 23, 1956[26].

The mission was clear: To ensure that atomic energy would be used to promote "peace, health, and prosperity throughout the world,[27]" while safeguarding against any military use. The establishment of the IAEA marked a

---

[26] https://www.iaea.org/about/overview/history
[27] https://www.iaea.org/about/overview/history

pivotal moment in international diplomacy, a hopeful experiment in global cooperation, and an effort to prevent the descent into nuclear anarchy.

The **nuclear arms race** between the United States and the Soviet Union was the theme that exhibited the future of the Cold War era. In **1949**, the Soviet Union tested its first atomic bomb, ending the United States' monopoly on nuclear weapons and intensifying the arms competition. Both nations rapidly expanded their arsenals, developing more powerful hydrogen bombs and delivery systems, including intercontinental ballistic missiles (ICBMs).

This competition was not just about military superiority but also ideological dominance. The United States and the Soviet Union sought to showcase their respective political systems—capitalism and communism—as the superior model for global development. The establishment of the IAEA can be seen as part of this broader context, where both superpowers aimed to influence the direction of nuclear technology and its applications worldwide.

The IAEA's creation was also influenced by the process of **decolonization** and the emergence of new nations seeking to assert their sovereignty and development agendas. These countries were wary of a new form of "atomic colonialism," where nuclear technology could become another tool for domination by the superpowers[28]. Therefore, they advocated for an

---

[28] https://issforum.org/articlereviews/66-iaea

international agency that would ensure equitable access to nuclear technology for peaceful purposes while preventing its misuse for military ends.

In summary, the establishment of the IAEA was a response to the complex interplay of scientific innovation, geopolitical rivalry, and the aspirations of newly independent nations. It represented a collective effort to harness the potential of nuclear energy for the common good while mitigating the risks associated with its destructive power.

The Founding Members and Global Expansion

The establishment of the International Atomic Energy Agency (IAEA) in 1957 marked a pivotal moment in international collaboration on nuclear energy. The agency's formation required ratification from at least 18 nations, including key nuclear powers of the time:

- United States

- Soviet Union (USSR)

- United Kingdom

- France

- Canada

The United States, under President Dwight D. Eisenhower, was instrumental in advocating for the peaceful use of atomic energy. Eisenhower's 1953 "Atoms for Peace" speech laid the groundwork for the IAEA's creation.

Initially sceptical about international oversight of nuclear technology, the Soviet Union's stance evolved to support the IAEA's formation. Premier Nikita Khrushchev recognized the potential of nuclear energy for peaceful purposes, stating:

"If nuclear energy is to be a force of progress, it must be placed in the service of humanity, not in the hands of imperialists seeking war."

The United Kingdom viewed the IAEA as a means to promote international cooperation and prevent nuclear proliferation. In 1957, the UK government expressed its support:

"We see in the IAEA not only a safeguard against proliferation but an instrument for international progress, ensuring that nuclear energy will power our future, not endanger it."

France, as a burgeoning nuclear power, recognized the importance of a global framework to oversee nuclear activities. French officials emphasized the need for an international body to balance national interests with global security.

Canada's involvement was pivotal, given its significant uranium resources and commitment to peaceful nuclear research. The nation saw the IAEA as a platform to share nuclear technology responsibly while preventing its misuse.

Germany: West Germany joined the IAEA in 1957, aligning with Western nations to promote peaceful nuclear cooperation. East Germany became a member later, reflecting the geopolitical divisions of the time.

China: Initially hesitant about international controls, China joined the IAEA in 1984 as its nuclear strategy evolved.

While the IAEA boasts near-universal membership, a few notable countries remain outside its framework:

- North Korea: Joined the IAEA in 1974 but withdrew in 1994 amid concerns over its nuclear weapons program.

- Israel: Maintains a policy of nuclear ambiguity and has not officially joined the IAEA, citing regional security concerns.

The IAEA's founding members laid the foundation for an international system aimed at promoting the peaceful use of nuclear energy while preventing its proliferation for military purposes. Their collective vision continues to influence global nuclear policy today, which as of 15th November 2024 included 180 members[29].

---

[29] https://www.iaea.org/about/governance/list-of-member-states

The IAEA's Mission: Peace, Health, and Prosperity

The International Atomic Energy Agency (IAEA) operates under a mission defined by its Statute, focusing on two primary objectives:

Promoting the Peaceful Use of Nuclear Technology: The IAEA seeks to "accelerate and enlarge the contribution of atomic energy to peace, health, and prosperity throughout the world".

Preventing Nuclear Weapons Proliferation: The agency ensures that its assistance is "not used in such a way as to further any military purpose[30]".

To fulfil these objectives, the IAEA undertakes several key functions:

- **Encouraging Research and Development**: The agency promotes scientific studies in nuclear energy to foster innovation and practical applications.

- **Providing Materials and Services**: It secures and supplies materials, services, equipment, and facilities to member states to support their nuclear initiatives.

---

[30] IAEA statue

- **Facilitating Information Exchange and Training**: The IAEA fosters the exchange of scientific and technical information and offers training programs to enhance global nuclear expertise.

Key Objectives of the IAEA:

Advancing Nuclear Science: The IAEA supports research in various fields, including medicine, agriculture, and industry, to harness nuclear technology for societal benefit.

Strengthening Nuclear Safety: The agency establishes global standards for reactor safety and radiation protection to ensure the secure operation of nuclear facilities.

Preventing Nuclear Proliferation: Through monitoring and verification, the IAEA ensures compliance with international agreements to prevent the misuse of nuclear materials.

Facilitating Nuclear Power Development: The agency assists nations in integrating nuclear energy into their infrastructure, providing guidance on safe and efficient practices.

Enhancing Climate Change Mitigation: The IAEA promotes nuclear energy as a low-carbon alternative to fossil fuels, contributing to global efforts to reduce greenhouse gas emissions.

In summary, the IAEA's mission encompasses promoting the peaceful applications of nuclear technology while implementing safeguards to prevent its diversion to military uses. Through its comprehensive programs, the agency aims to harness nuclear science for the betterment of humanity, ensuring safety, security, and sustainability

Membership Obligations: Responsibilities of IAEA States

The International Atomic Energy Agency (IAEA) operates on the principle of **sovereign equality**—every member state, regardless of its nuclear capabilities, must adhere to a set of responsibilities enshrined in the IAEA Statute. These obligations ensure that nuclear energy remains a force for peace, development, and security rather than a tool for destruction.

Nuclear Non-Proliferation and Safeguards: The Watchful Eye of the IAEA

At the heart of the IAEA's mission is nuclear non-proliferation, ensuring that nuclear materials and technology are used only for peaceful purposes. To this end, every member state must accept the agency's safeguards agreements as outlined in Article III of the IAEA Statute. These safeguards serve as a global verification system, ensuring compliance with international nuclear treaties—most notably the Treaty on the Non-Proliferation of Nuclear Weapons (NPT).

On-Site Inspections: Preventing the Misuse of Nuclear Materials

The IAEA is empowered to conduct on-site inspections, audits, and monitoring to verify that nuclear materials are not diverted for military use. These inspections include:

- Unannounced visits to nuclear facilities.

- Analysis of nuclear fuel samples to detect any irregularities.

- Remote surveillance using cameras and sensors placed at key nuclear sites.

- Cross-checking national reports submitted by member states with independently gathered data.

As per Article XII of the IAEA Statute, if the agency detects non-compliance, it can report the violation to the United Nations Security Council and General Assembly, potentially leading to diplomatic action or sanctions.

A Historical Example: The IAEA's inspections played a crucial role in revealing Iraq's secret nuclear weapons program in the 1990s, which led to UN sanctions and disarmament efforts. Similarly, ongoing IAEA monitoring of Iran's nuclear activities under the Joint Comprehensive Plan of Action (JCPOA) underscores its critical role in global security.

Financial Contributions: Funding the Global Nuclear Watchdog

Just as every nation contributes to the United Nations, IAEA members financially support the agency's operations based on an assessment scale. This is outlined in Article XIV of the IAEA Statute, which specifies two categories of funding:

1. Administrative Budget – Covers the cost of staff, research, training programs, and nuclear safety initiatives.

2. Operational Budget – Funds nuclear assistance programs, technology transfers, and inspections.

The largest financial contributors are typically the United States, China, Russia, Japan, and the European Union. Developing countries receive assistance through the IAEA's Technical Cooperation Program, ensuring equitable access to nuclear technology for energy, medicine, and agriculture. The agency can also accept voluntary contributions to fund specific nuclear projects, such as climate change mitigation efforts and cancer treatment programs.

Every year, the IAEA submits a budget report to the General Conference, where member states vote on the agency's financial plans. This process ensures accountability and international oversight.

Commitment to Peaceful Use: The Global Trust Pact

Article IV of the IAEA Statute emphasizes that all members must commit to using nuclear energy for peaceful applications. This includes:

- **Transparency in National Nuclear Programs**: Members must report their nuclear activities and allow IAEA monitoring.

- **Compliance with IAEA Regulations**: Countries must implement IAEA safety and security standards in their nuclear facilities, preventing accidents and illicit nuclear trafficking.

- **Preventing the Spread of Sensitive Nuclear Technology**: Members are prohibited from transferring nuclear weapons-related knowledge to non-nuclear-weapon states or non-state actors.

When a country fails to comply with these obligations, the IAEA can refer the matter to the United Nations Security Council. Notable cases include:

- North Korea: Withdrew from the IAEA in 1994 after refusing to comply with nuclear inspections and later conducted nuclear tests.

- Iran: Has been under IAEA scrutiny for uranium enrichment activities that could lead to weapons development.

By enforcing these commitments, the IAEA acts as a global nuclear watchdog, ensuring that atomic energy remains a tool for progress, not a weapon of destruction.

The role of IAEA in 21st century comparing to 20th century

The International Atomic Energy Agency (IAEA) has evolved significantly from its mid-20th-century origins, adapting to the dynamic challenges and opportunities of the 21st century. Initially established to promote peaceful nuclear applications and prevent weapons proliferation, the IAEA's role has expanded to address contemporary issues such as climate change, nuclear security, and technological innovation.

Nuclear Energy and Climate Change

In the 20th century, the IAEA primarily focused on facilitating the peaceful use of nuclear technology, emphasizing energy production, medical applications, and agricultural advancements. Today, with the global imperative to reduce carbon emissions, nuclear power has re-emerged as a pivotal component in achieving Net Zero goals. The 2022 IAEA International Ministerial Conference underscored this transition, stating:

"Nuclear power is currently the only low-carbon technology that can provide electricity and heat at scale... All energy sectors must reach net zero, and nuclear energy is an essential part of that transition."

This perspective highlights nuclear energy's unique capacity to deliver consistent, large-scale, low-carbon power, complementing renewable sources like wind and solar.

Nuclear Safety and Security

The IAEA's commitment to nuclear safety has deepened over the decades. The 1986 Chernobyl disaster and the 2011 Fukushima incident prompted the agency to enhance global safety standards and emergency preparedness. In the 21st century, the IAEA continues to play a critical role in safeguarding nuclear facilities, especially in conflict zones. The ongoing situation in Ukraine, particularly around the Zaporizhzhia Nuclear Power Plant, has tested the agency's ability to ensure nuclear safety during armed conflicts. IAEA Director General Rafael Grossi emphasized the importance of maintaining nuclear safety standards amidst geopolitical tensions:

"We are living in unprecedented times, where the threat of nuclear incidents is at its highest since the Cold War[31]."

---

[31] https://www.wsj.com/world/russia/nuclear-war-risks-rise-again-stoked-by-global-conflicts-fa3333b6

Technological Innovation and Non-Proliferation

The IAEA has embraced technological advancements to enhance its monitoring and verification capabilities. The integration of satellite imagery, remote sensors, and data analytics has improved the agency's ability to detect unauthorized nuclear activities. However, challenges persist, as geopolitical conflicts and technological proliferation test the robustness of the non-proliferation regime.

The erosion of key arms control treaties and the modernization of nuclear arsenals by major powers have raised concerns about a potential new arms race[32]. Rafael Grossi, director general of the International Atomic Energy Agency, spoke after visiting the plant in the Kursk region, where Ukrainian forces pierced the border in a lightning incursion on 6th Aug 2024 and Russia is still battling to eject them: *"This means that the core of the reactor containing nuclear material is protected just by a normal roof. This makes it extremely exposed and fragile, for example, to an artillery impact or a drone or a missile,"* he said. "So this is why we believe that a nuclear power plant of this type, so close to a point of contact or a military front, is an extremely serious fact that we take very seriously[33]"

---

[32] https://www.wsj.com/world/russia/nuclear-war-risks-rise-again-stoked-by-global-conflicts-fa3333b6
[33] https://www.reuters.com/world/europe/un-nuclear-chief-visit-russian-atomic-plant-near-front-line-2024-08-27/

The global nuclear non-proliferation regime is under unprecedented pressure, with countries openly debating the development of atomic weapons.

The IAEA's role in the 21st century has expanded beyond its original mandate, adapting to address the intertwined challenges of energy security, climate change, and geopolitical instability. By promoting safe and peaceful nuclear technology, the agency continues to be a cornerstone of international efforts to harness atomic energy responsibly, ensuring that it contributes to global peace, health, and prosperity.

Superpowers and the IAEA: A Legacy of Rivalry, Cooperation, and Control

The **United States** and the **Soviet Union** were not just founding members of the International Atomic Energy Agency (IAEA)—they were its architects, its challengers, and at times, its adversaries. Their nuclear ambitions and geopolitical rivalry shaped the very foundation of the IAEA, as they sought to balance **nuclear power's promise and peril** on the world stage.

From Cold War confrontations to diplomatic breakthroughs, the history of the **IAEA is a testament to their struggle for dominance, their reluctant cooperation, and their ultimate recognition that nuclear energy could not be left unchecked**. The following key events highlight their influence on the agency's evolution:

The Baruch Plan (1946): A Vision That Never Took Flight

Before the IAEA existed, the United States sought to **seize the initiative on nuclear control**. In 1946, U.S. diplomat **Bernard Baruch** presented a radical proposal to the United Nations:

"We are here to make a choice between the quick and the dead... We must elect world peace or world destruction." — Bernard Baruch, 1946

The **Baruch Plan** called for placing all **nuclear materials and research under international control** to prevent an arms race. But the **Soviet Union** saw it as an attempt to **lock in America's nuclear monopoly** and refused to agree unless the U.S. first **destroyed its atomic arsenal**. The deadlock **paved the way for the Cold War and the nuclear arms race**, showing the world just how difficult it was to regulate atomic power.

The Birth of the IAEA (1957): Superpowers Find Common Ground

As the Cold War intensified, both superpowers recognized that nuclear technology could not remain **entirely unregulated**. Despite deep mistrust, the U.S. and the USSR **agreed on the need for an international**

agency to promote the **peaceful use of nuclear energy while preventing its misuse.**

Thus, in **1957**, the IAEA was born, with its Statute emphasizing:

"The Agency shall seek to accelerate and enlarge the contribution of atomic energy to peace, health, and prosperity throughout the world."

Though the **IAEA's headquarters were placed in Vienna**, both superpowers remained highly involved— each trying to **ensure that nuclear governance did not tilt in the other's favour.**

The McCloy–Zorin Accords (1961): A Pledge to Prevent Nuclear Catastrophe

By the 1960s, the arms race had reached terrifying proportions. The United States and the Soviet Union held **enough nuclear firepower to destroy the world many times over.** Yet, amidst the tensions, a rare moment of **cooperation** emerged in 1961 when the two nations signed the **McCloy–Zorin Accords**, committing to:

- **Work toward complete nuclear disarmament**

- **Strengthen international safeguards** against nuclear weapons

- **Use the IAEA as a mechanism for oversight**

Though largely symbolic, this agreement **laid the groundwork for future arms control talks** and reaffirmed the IAEA's role in monitoring compliance.

The Nuclear Non-Proliferation Treaty (NPT) (1968): The IAEA's Greatest Responsibility

Recognizing the growing threat of nuclear proliferation, the U.S. and the USSR led negotiations for the **Nuclear Non-Proliferation Treaty (NPT)** in **1968**. The treaty aimed to:

- **Prevent new countries from acquiring nuclear weapons**

- **Promote peaceful nuclear technology under IAEA supervision**

- **Encourage disarmament among nuclear-armed nations**

The IAEA became the **treaty's verification body,** tasked with **inspecting nuclear programs and ensuring compliance**. This marked a defining moment in the agency's history, elevating it to the role of **global nuclear watchdog**.

The Chernobyl Disaster (1986): A Wake-Up Call for Global Nuclear Safety

For decades, nuclear energy had been a symbol of **progress and power**. But the **Chernobyl disaster** in 1986 shattered that illusion.

When **Reactor 4 at the Chernobyl Nuclear Power Plant exploded**, sending radioactive material across Europe, the world witnessed firsthand the dangers of **poorly regulated nuclear technology**. The Soviet Union initially **downplayed the disaster**, but the IAEA's international experts were brought in to **assess the damage and improve global safety standards**.

This event **reshaped the agency's focus**, leading to:

- **Stronger international safety regulations**

- **Emergency response protocols for nuclear accidents**

- **New transparency rules for nuclear-armed states**

IAEA Director General **Hans Blix** declared in the aftermath:

"Chernobyl was a turning point. Nuclear energy, once thought to be solely a symbol of progress, became a matter of survival and accountability.[34]**"**

---

[34] reuters.com/world/europe/key-facts-chornobyl-nuclear-plant-2025-02-14

Superpower Influence: From Cold War Tensions to Modern-Day Challenges

Although the **Cold War ended in 1991**, the influence of the U.S. and Russia (the Soviet Union's successor) over the IAEA **remains strong**. Both nations continue to **fund, monitor, and shape nuclear policy** through the agency.

New Challenges in the 21st Century:

- **Iran's nuclear program**: The IAEA remains at the center of monitoring Iran's nuclear activities amid international tensions.

- **North Korea's withdrawal from the IAEA (1994)**: North Korea expelled IAEA inspectors and later conducted nuclear tests, challenging global non-proliferation efforts.

- **The Ukraine conflict (2022–present)**: Russia's military actions near **Zaporizhzhia Nuclear Power Plant** raised fears of nuclear catastrophe, testing the IAEA's ability to operate in war zones.

Chapter conclusion: A Legacy That Shapes the Future

The United States and the Soviet Union were the driving forces behind the creation of the IAEA, each attempting to use it as a tool for global influence. But what began as a product of Cold War rivalry and suspicion has become one of the world's most essential institutions for nuclear safety and security.

Today, as the world grapples with climate change, nuclear security, and energy crises, the IAEA's mission is more relevant than ever. The superpowers that once competed for dominance now find themselves in a world where cooperation—not conflict—is the only path forward.

"The power of the atom is a double-edged sword. Our duty is to ensure it lights up cities, not destroys them." — IAEA Director General Rafael Grossi.

The IAEA's story is far from over. Its greatest challenges—and its greatest achievements—may still lie ahead.

Chapter (3)

The Limited Test Ban Treaty of 1963 – A Step Away from the Nuclear Abyss

"An important first step--a step towards peace--a step towards reason--a step away from war"

John F. Kennedy (U.S. President)

A World on the Brink: The Road to the Limited Test Ban Treaty

As the world emerged from the devastation of World War II, it entered a new and terrifying age—the atomic age. The nuclear mushroom clouds over Hiroshima and Nagasaki in August 1945 were more than the end of a war; they marked the beginning of a precarious future where mankind wielded the power to destroy itself.

The postwar era quickly descended into an ideological battle between the United States and the Soviet Union, a conflict fought not just with words and proxy wars, but with an escalating arms race. By the 1950s, the race was no longer limited to who could build the most bombs but who could build the most powerful. The development of the hydrogen bomb in the early 1950s by both superpowers only intensified global anxieties.

Yet, even as nuclear arsenals grew, so did public awareness of the dangers of radioactive fallout. Scientists warned of the genetic damage caused by nuclear tests, and worldwide protests emerged. Citizens, activists, and leaders alike began to recognize the need for some form of control before the nuclear genie could no longer be contained.

The Growing Call for Action

The first serious discussions about limiting nuclear testing began within the United Nations Disarmament Commission in 1955. The Subcommittee of Five—comprising the United States, the United Kingdom, Canada, France, and the Soviet Union—was tasked with negotiating a nuclear test ban. Over the next eight years, however, progress remained sluggish. Verification of nuclear tests and Cold War tensions repeatedly stalled negotiations. By the late 1950s and early 1960s, however, the political climate was shifting. The terrifying near-miss of the Cuban Missile Crisis in October 1962 brought humanity to the edge of nuclear war, serving as a stark reminder that an unchecked arms race could have catastrophic consequences.

It was within this climate of urgency that diplomacy took center stage. U.S. President John F. Kennedy, British Prime Minister Harold Macmillan, and Soviet Premier Nikita Khrushchev recognized the need for de-escalation. In mid-1963, direct negotiations between Washington, London, and Moscow intensified, culminating in the drafting of the Limited Test Ban Treaty (LTBT).

The Role of Public and Scientific Advocacy

The Limited Test Ban Treaty was not merely the result of diplomatic efforts; it was strongly influenced by public pressure and scientific research. Throughout the 1950s and early 1960s, growing evidence of radioactive contamination fueled global protests. Scientists, including Linus Pauling, repeatedly warned of the long-term effects of radioactive fallout on human health and genetics.

The global anti-nuclear movement, spearheaded by organizations such as the Campaign for Nuclear Disarmament (CND) and Women Strike for Peace, put immense pressure on governments to halt nuclear testing. The combination of scientific evidence and public activism made it increasingly difficult for world leaders to ignore the issue.

The IAEA and Nuclear Test Ban Verification

The establishment of the International Atomic Energy Agency (IAEA) in 1957 was a crucial development in ensuring peaceful nuclear cooperation and preventing nuclear proliferation. While the IAEA was not directly responsible for enforcing the LTBT, its role in nuclear verification became critical in subsequent treaties.

The IAEA's safeguard agreements under the Nuclear Non-Proliferation Treaty (NPT) helped monitor compliance with nuclear restrictions and deter violations. As arms control agreements expanded in the following decades, the IAEA's expertise in monitoring nuclear programs played an integral part in the global efforts to limit the spread of nuclear weapons.

The Limited Test Ban Treaty of 1963 was a turning point in global arms control efforts. It reflected a growing realization that nuclear war was not winnable, and that some constraints on nuclear testing were necessary to preserve human life and the environment.

While the treaty did not end the nuclear arms race, it demonstrated that international diplomacy and public advocacy could lead to concrete progress in controlling the spread of nuclear weapons. The IAEA's expanding role in subsequent years further solidified the global commitment to nuclear safety and non-proliferation.

The LTBT's legacy endures today, influencing contemporary discussions on nuclear disarmament and climate change, as nations continue to grapple with the challenges of nuclear energy, security, and international stability.

The Signing of the Treaty: A Turning Point

On **August 5, 1963**, the **Limited Test Ban Treaty** was signed in Moscow by representatives of the three major nuclear powers:

- **United States:** Secretary of State **Dean Rusk**

- **United Kingdom:** Foreign Secretary **Sir Douglas Home**

- **Soviet Union:** Foreign Minister **Andrei Gromyko**

Following its approval by the U.S. Senate, the treaty officially came into effect on **October 10, 1963**. John F. Kennedy (U.S. President) articulated his views on the treaty: *" This treaty is not the millennium. It will not resolve all conflicts, or cause the Communists to forego their ambitions, or eliminate the dangers of war. It will not reduce our need for arms or allies or programs of assistance to others. But it is an important first step--a step towards peace--a step towards reason--a step away from war[35]."*

---

[35] https://www.jfklibrary.org/archives/other-resources/john-f-kennedy-speeches/nuclear-test-ban-treaty-19630726

Purpose and Objectives of the Limited Test Ban Treaty (LTBT)

The Limited Test Ban Treaty (LTBT) of 1963 was a pioneering agreement in arms control, marking a critical step toward reducing the dangers associated with nuclear weapons testing. The treaty sought to mitigate the escalating environmental and geopolitical threats posed by nuclear weapons tests. The primary goals of the LTBT were:

Reducing Environmental Contamination

One of the treaty's foremost aims was to eliminate radioactive fallout from nuclear testing in the atmosphere, outer space, and underwater, which had been increasingly polluting the environment. The 1950s and early 1960s saw extensive nuclear testing, releasing radioactive isotopes like Strontium-90 and Cesium-137, which contaminated food supplies, water, and ecosystems worldwide.

Preventing the Spread of Radioactive Fallout and Global Health Risks

Scientists and health experts, including the renowned physicist Linus Pauling, warned of the severe consequences of radioactive fallout, including genetic mutations, cancer, and birth defects. Studies showed that nuclear tests were contaminating regions far beyond test sites, prompting widespread public outcry and fueling movements like the Campaign for Nuclear Disarmament (CND).

Slowing the Nuclear Arms Race

By limiting nations' ability to conduct atmospheric tests, the treaty aimed to curb the advancement of nuclear weapon technology. While underground tests continued, banning atmospheric tests hindered efforts to develop and perfect more powerful nuclear weapons, slowing the pace of the Cold War arms race between the United States and the Soviet Union.

Encouraging Future Arms Control Agreements

The LTBT was designed to lay the groundwork for broader non-proliferation efforts. It demonstrated that diplomatic agreements on nuclear weapons control were possible and set the stage for later treaties, such as the Nuclear Non-Proliferation Treaty (NPT) of 1968, the Threshold Test Ban Treaty of 1974, and eventually the Comprehensive Nuclear-Test-Ban Treaty (CTBT) of 1996, which sought to ban all nuclear tests, including underground detonations.

Obligations and Commitments of Member States

Under the LTBT, all signatory nations agreed to abide by strict prohibitions on nuclear testing in designated environments. The treaty's legal framework, outlined in Article I, detailed the commitments required of signatories. Key Commitments of LTBT Signatories

Prohibit Nuclear Explosions in the Atmosphere, Outer Space, and Underwater

Article I explicitly states that signatories must "prohibit, prevent, and not carry out any nuclear weapon test explosion, or any other nuclear explosion" in these three environments.

Prevent Radioactive Contamination Beyond National Borders

The treaty did not completely ban nuclear testing, but it sought to contain its effects. Article I, Section (b) specifies that nuclear tests conducted underground would only be permissible if they did not cause radioactive debris to extend beyond the borders of the country conducting the test.

Refrain from Assisting or Encouraging Nuclear Testing by Other Nations

Article I, Section 2 requires signatories to not aid, encourage, or participate in nuclear testing conducted by any other state. This was a crucial measure aimed at preventing nuclear proliferation by ensuring that signatories did not indirectly support tests conducted by non-signatories.

Allow for Treaty Amendments and Future Expansions

Article II of the treaty provides a framework for proposing and adopting amendments. If one-third or more of the parties request a conference to discuss amendments, the Depositary Governments (United States, United Kingdom, and the Soviet Union) are required to convene a formal meeting to discuss modifications.

While the LTBT was a significant milestone in arms control, it had notable loopholes and limitations:

- Underground nuclear tests were not banned, meaning that nuclear powers continued testing at reduced frequencies, particularly through the 1970s and 1980s. The treaty did not establish an international verification system, making enforcement largely dependent on trust and voluntary compliance.

- France and China refused to sign the treaty in 1963 and continued nuclear testing well into the 1990s, reducing its effectiveness as a global measure.

- It did not include binding enforcement mechanisms, unlike later treaties such as the Comprehensive Nuclear-Test-Ban Treaty (CTBT), which introduced a verification system using seismic monitoring and satellite surveillance.

Despite its limitations, the LTBT represented a turning point in international efforts to control nuclear weapons proliferation. It was the first formal agreement between nuclear-armed states to limit nuclear testing, setting a precedent for subsequent arms control treaties.

By reducing the environmental and health hazards of atmospheric nuclear tests, the treaty helped mitigate the global impact of nuclear fallout. It also eased Cold War tensions, proving that the United States and the Soviet Union could cooperate on nuclear issues despite their broader geopolitical rivalry.

The LTBT's legacy endures today, influencing contemporary discussions on nuclear disarmament, environmental protection, and the role of international law in arms control. Its principles continue to inform modern non-proliferation agreements, ensuring that nuclear testing remains a key focus in global security efforts.

The Enduring Legacy of the Limited Test Ban Treaty: Compliance, Challenges, and Future Prospects

The Limited Test Ban Treaty (LTBT) was a landmark agreement that laid the foundation for modern nuclear arms control. Over time, more than 125 countries signed the treaty, solidifying its status as a crucial step in reducing the dangers of nuclear testing. However, not all nuclear powers embraced it. France and China initially refused to join, choosing instead to continue their nuclear testing programs well into the late 20th century.

Despite evolving political landscapes and advances in nuclear technology, no major signatory nation has ever officially withdrawn from the LTBT. However, periodic tensions surrounding new weapons technologies and shifting global security dynamics have tested the treaty's effectiveness. While nations have largely adhered to its restrictions, concerns over nuclear modernization and potential loopholes continue to surface.

The LTBT's Role in Shaping Future Agreements

Far from being an isolated agreement, the LTBT became a stepping stone for more ambitious non-proliferation efforts. It directly influenced the Nuclear Non-Proliferation Treaty (NPT) of 1968, which established a framework for preventing the spread of nuclear weapons, and later, the Comprehensive Nuclear-Test-Ban Treaty (CTBT) of 1996, which sought to prohibit all nuclear explosions, including those underground. However, the CTBT has yet to fully take effect, as key nations— including the United States, China, India, and Pakistan— have not ratified it, preventing its full implementation.

The Limited Test Ban Treaty remains in force and continues to play a vital role in global arms control. While it does not prevent all forms of nuclear testing, it stands as a symbol of diplomatic progress, reminding the world of the importance of international cooperation in limiting nuclear threats. Despite the challenges posed by evolving military technologies and geopolitical tensions, the LTBT's legacy endures, reinforcing the idea that global security is best achieved through collective restraint and dialogue

Chapter conclusion: A Step Toward a Safer World

While the LTBT was a historic breakthrough, it had significant limitations. The treaty did not stop the arms race—nuclear tests continued underground, and nations found new ways to advance their nuclear arsenals. Moreover, not all nuclear powers joined the treaty, with France and China refusing to sign at the time, continuing their nuclear testing programs.

Nevertheless, the LTBT laid the groundwork for future arms control agreements, including the Nuclear Non-Proliferation Treaty (NPT) of 1968, the Threshold Test Ban Treaty of 1974, and eventually the Comprehensive Nuclear-Test-Ban Treaty (CTBT) of 1996, which sought to ban all nuclear explosions.

While the world remains fraught with nuclear tensions, the treaty's legacy endures—a testament to what diplomacy can achieve even in the darkest of times. As President Kennedy aptly put it the treaty is not the millennium, but it is an important first step—a step towards a more peaceful world.

Chapter (4)

The Treaty on the Non-Proliferation of Nuclear Weapons (NPT)

*"The United States is not asking any country to accept any
safeguards that we are not willing to accept ourselves"*

Lyndon B. Johnson (U.S. President)

Background and Historical Context

By the mid-20th century, the world stood at the precipice
of nuclear catastrophe. The devastating bombings of
Hiroshima and Nagasaki in 1945 had demonstrated the
unprecedented destructive power of nuclear weapons,
ushering in an era of fear and geopolitical competition. In
the years that followed, the Cold War rivalry between the
United States and the Soviet Union escalated into an
uncontrolled nuclear arms race, with both superpowers
amassing thousands of nuclear warheads in a precarious
struggle for strategic supremacy.

The first significant attempt to manage the nuclear threat
came in 1957, with the establishment of the International

Atomic Energy Agency (IAEA). Founded under the auspices of the United Nations, the IAEA was designed to promote the peaceful use of nuclear energy while ensuring that nuclear technology was not diverted to weapons development. The organization's creation was heavily influenced by U.S. President Dwight D. Eisenhower's 1953 speech, *Atoms for Peace*, in which he proposed international cooperation to harness nuclear energy for constructive purposes rather than military destruction.

While the IAEA introduced safeguards and monitoring mechanisms, it did not directly prevent the continued proliferation of nuclear weapons. The United States, the Soviet Union, the United Kingdom, France, and China all developed nuclear arsenals, and concern grew that other countries, too, would seek to join the exclusive nuclear club.

Despite the IAEA's efforts, nuclear tensions continued to rise. The late 1950s and early 1960s saw numerous atmospheric and underground nuclear tests, intensifying public fears of radioactive fallout and environmental catastrophe. To address these concerns, the Limited Test Ban Treaty (LTBT) was signed in 1963 by the United States, the Soviet Union, and the United Kingdom, banning nuclear tests in the atmosphere, outer space, and underwater. This treaty was an essential first step toward nuclear restraint, but it did not limit the production or possession of nuclear weapons.

At the same time, the Cuban Missile Crisis of 1962 brought the world to the brink of nuclear war. The crisis began when U.S. reconnaissance aircraft discovered Soviet ballistic missiles in Cuba, just 90 miles off the U.S. coast. For thirteen days, the world watched as the two superpowers engaged in a tense diplomatic standoff, with both sides preparing for a possible nuclear conflict. President John F. Kennedy and Soviet Premier Nikita Khrushchev ultimately reached a last-minute agreement, with the Soviets withdrawing their missiles from Cuba in exchange for a U.S. pledge not to invade Cuba and a secret agreement to remove U.S. missiles from Turkey.

The Cuban Missile Crisis had a profound impact on nuclear diplomacy. It exposed the fragility of global security and made it clear that, without serious arms control measures, future crises could spiral into full-scale nuclear war. Both the United States and the Soviet Union recognized the urgent need for formal agreements to regulate nuclear weapons development and proliferation.

The Birth of the NPT

Following the Cuban crisis, nuclear non-proliferation became a top priority for world leaders. The United Nations, under increasing pressure from the international community, began facilitating discussions on a comprehensive treaty that would prevent the spread of nuclear weapons. These discussions gained momentum in the mid-1960s, culminating in the drafting of the Treaty on the Non-Proliferation of Nuclear Weapons (NPT).

Negotiations were led primarily by the United States and the Soviet Union, who, despite their rivalry, recognized that a world with more nuclear-armed states would only increase global instability. The treaty was designed to strike a balance between nuclear disarmament, non-proliferation, and the peaceful use of nuclear energy.

On July 1, 1968, the United States, the Soviet Union, and the United Kingdom signed the NPT in London, Moscow, and Washington, officially opening it for signature. The treaty entered into force on March 5, 1970, and became one of the most significant international agreements in the nuclear age, setting the foundation for modern nuclear arms control efforts.

Who Signed the Treaty? Key Parties and Their Positions

At its inception, the NPT was signed by 93 countries, including the three nuclear superpowers of the time: the United States, the Soviet Union, and the United Kingdom . Over time, 191 states joined the treaty, making it one of the most widely adhered-to international agreements in history.

The United States, a Clear Vision of To Avoid Nuclear Proliferation

The U.S. position on the NPT was clear from the outset: to limit the spread of nuclear weapons while maintaining its own nuclear arsenal for deterrence. During the signing, President Lyndon B. Johnson stated: *"the treaty that prevents the spread of nuclear weapons ... the United States is not asking any country to accept any safeguards that we are not willing to accept ourselves [36]."*

The U.S. pledged to work toward nuclear disarmament but maintained its nuclear stockpile as a necessary counterbalance during the Cold War.

The Soviet Union: A Tense Debate Behind the Nuclear Non-Proliferation Treaty

For the Soviet Union, the NPT was both a security measure and a diplomatic manoeuvre. Soviet leader Leonid Brezhnev emphasized the need to stop nuclear proliferation, particularly to West Germany and other U.S. allies, while ensuring that the Soviet nuclear arsenal remained formidable.

However, within the Soviet sphere of influence, not all allies were convinced. Romania, led by Nicolae Ceaușescu and Ion Gheorghe Maurer, emerged as a major critic of

---

[36] https://www.presidency.ucsb.edu/documents/remarks-the-signing-the-nuclear-nonproliferation-treaty

the proposed treaty. In a series of high-stakes meetings with Soviet leaders Leonid Brezhnev and Alexei Kosygin, the Romanians voiced concerns that the NPT was not a genuine step toward disarmament but rather a mechanism to maintain the nuclear monopoly of a few powerful states.

During a pivotal meeting in March 1967, Ceaușescu made his stance clear. *"Steps for the non-proliferation of nuclear weapons need to be tied more to overall steps on disarmament*[37]*"* he argued, warning that the treaty would solidify inequality between nuclear and non-nuclear states. He accused the United States of using the treaty as a tool to dominate smaller nations, referring to its actions in Vietnam: *"American imperialism is worse than a wolf."*

The Soviets, however, viewed the treaty as a critical tool to restrain nuclear ambitions in the West, particularly in West Germany. Brezhnev insisted, *"This treaty is mainly directed against Federal Republic of Germany, against the countries in the NATO bloc,"* arguing that preventing Bonn from acquiring nuclear weapons was paramount.

Despite this, Romania was not convinced. Maurer pointedly remarked, *"At least our hands will not be tied,"* a statement that suggested Romania was unwilling to completely shut the door on developing its own nuclear capability in the future. Brezhnev, seemingly alarmed,

---

[37] Record of Conversations in the CPSU with N. Ceausescu and I.G. Maurer, 17-18 March 1967

responded, *"Cde. Maurer is saying: 'At least our hands won't be tied!' I do not know how to understand this[38]."*

By March 1968, when the treaty had evolved to include additional provisions on nuclear safeguards and disarmament commitments, Romania still resisted. Ceaușescu proposed additional guarantees, including stronger security assurances for non-nuclear states. However, the Soviets had already invested too much in the treaty to reopen negotiations. Kosygin, frustrated, delivered a pointed warning: *"You are calling on us to [join] the struggle, you are saying that we should fight. We have fought for a long time, and we know what struggle is. We do not need to be called upon to do this. We fight not in word but in deed, we do not use broad statements ….If one tightens the screw to the limit and then continues trying to tighten it even further, then one might strip the thread."*

In the end, Romania refused to endorse the treaty in full, standing apart from its Warsaw Pact allies. The tense exchanges between the Soviets and the Romanians underscored deeper fractures within the Eastern Bloc— fractures that would only grow in the years to come.

The United Kingdom, New Clear Powers, No More!

The United Kingdom, the third official nuclear-weapon state under the treaty, saw the NPT as a means to prevent

---

[38] Record of Conversations in the CPSU with N. Ceausescu and I.G. Maurer, 17-18 March 1967

smaller nations from acquiring nuclear capabilities. The British Foreign Office declared: *"The Treaty provides the best framework for preventing the spread of nuclear weapons and promoting peaceful nuclear cooperation."*

Purpose, Objectives, and Obligations Under the Treaty

The NPT is a landmark international treaty whose objective is to prevent the spread of nuclear weapons and weapons technology, to promote cooperation in the peaceful uses of nuclear energy and to further the goal of achieving nuclear disarmament and general and complete disarmament. The Treaty represents the only binding commitment in a multilateral treaty to the goal of disarmament by the nuclear-weapon States[39]. The NPT is built upon three central pillars:

- Non-Proliferation: Nuclear-armed states agreed not to transfer nuclear weapons or assist other nations in acquiring them. Non-nuclear states committed not to seek nuclear weapons.

- Disarmament: All parties pledged to pursue negotiations in good faith toward nuclear disarmament.

- Peaceful Use of Nuclear Energy: The treaty promotes the right of all signatories to develop

---

[39]https://disarmament.unoda.org/wmd/nuclear/npt/#:~:text=The%20NPT%20is%20a%20landmark,the%20five%20nuclear%2Dweapon%20States.

nuclear energy for peaceful purposes under strict International Atomic Energy Agency (IAEA) safeguards.

Key Provisions of the Treaty on the Non-Proliferation of Nuclear Weapons (NPT)

The Treaty on the Non-Proliferation of Nuclear Weapons (NPT) is built on a carefully crafted framework aimed at preventing nuclear proliferation, promoting disarmament, and ensuring the peaceful use of nuclear energy. Below is an examination of the key articles that form the backbone of the treaty, incorporating relevant amendments and subsequent international commitments.

Article I: Prohibition on Transfer of Nuclear Weapons and Technology

This article establishes a strict ban on nuclear-weapon states (the United States, Russia, China, France, and the United Kingdom) from transferring nuclear weapons, nuclear explosive devices, or related technologies to any recipient, whether directly or indirectly.

- Restrictions on Assistance: Nuclear-weapon states are also prohibited from assisting, encouraging, or inducing any non-nuclear-weapon state to develop nuclear weapons. This applies not only to physical transfers but also technical and scientific assistance that could contribute to weapons development.

- Expanded Verification: Over the years, UN Security Council resolutions (such as Resolution 1540 in 2004) have reinforced this commitment by mandating all states to prevent non-state actors (e.g., terrorist groups) from acquiring nuclear technology.

Article II: Commitment of Non-Nuclear States to Non-Proliferation

Under this provision, non-nuclear-weapon states agree not to seek, receive, or manufacture nuclear weapons or related explosive devices.

- Ban on Acquisition: This restriction applies to all forms of procurement, including direct development, indirect acquisition through illicit means, and even secret agreements with nuclear-armed states.

- Non-Proliferation Challenges: Despite this provision, some nations, such as India, Pakistan, and Israel, have remained outside the NPT framework and have since developed nuclear arsenals. North Korea, originally a signatory, withdrew in 2003 and has since conducted nuclear tests.

Article III: Establishment of IAEA Safeguards and Verification Mechanisms

To prevent the diversion of civilian nuclear technology to military use, this article mandates that non-nuclear-weapon states accept safeguards administered by the International Atomic Energy Agency (IAEA).

- Comprehensive Safeguards Agreements (CSAs): All non-nuclear states must conclude agreements with the IAEA to ensure their nuclear programs remain peaceful.

- Additional Protocol (1997): The Additional Protocol, a major amendment to the NPT safeguards regime, grants the IAEA enhanced inspection authority, allowing it to conduct short-notice inspections and demand more detailed reporting on nuclear activities.

- Verification Challenges: While IAEA safeguards have been largely successful, countries such as Iran and North Korea have challenged their authority, leading to prolonged diplomatic conflicts over nuclear compliance.

Article IV: The Right to Peaceful Nuclear Energy

This article recognizes the inalienable right of all state parties to conduct research, develop, and use nuclear energy for peaceful purposes.

- Promotion of Civilian Nuclear Power: The treaty obligates nuclear-armed states and other advanced nations to assist non-nuclear states in developing nuclear energy, provided it remains under strict IAEA monitoring.

- International Nuclear Cooperation: To facilitate this, organizations such as the IAEA and Nuclear Suppliers Group (NSG) oversee nuclear trade and technology sharing while preventing illicit proliferation.

- Tension Between Energy and Proliferation: Some states, such as Iran, have used this provision to justify the development of advanced nuclear enrichment capabilities, leading to concerns about dual-use technology (which could be diverted for weapons production).

Article VI: Commitment to Disarmament

This article serves as a legal commitment by all state parties, including nuclear-weapon states, to pursue negotiations on disarmament and the eventual elimination of nuclear weapons.

- Disarmament Challenges: Although the United States and Russia have significantly reduced their nuclear arsenals through agreements like START (Strategic Arms Reduction Treaty), complete disarmament remains elusive.

- Review Conferences: Every five years, NPT Review Conferences are held to evaluate progress on disarmament and non-proliferation goals.

- The Treaty on the Prohibition of Nuclear Weapons (TPNW) (2017): Frustrated by the slow progress on disarmament, 122 countries voted for the TPNW, which seeks to ban nuclear weapons outright. However, all five nuclear-weapon states boycotted the treaty, arguing that nuclear deterrence is still necessary for global security.

Article VII: Nuclear-Weapon-Free Zones (NWFZs)

- This article allows regional groups of states to form nuclear-weapon-free zones to enhance regional security.

- Major NWFZs exist in Latin America (Treaty of Tlatelolco), Africa (Pelindaba Treaty), and Southeast Asia (Bangkok Treaty).

Article VIII: Treaty Amendments and Review Mechanism

- Any state party may propose amendments to the treaty.

- The NPT Review Conference, held every five years, serves as the primary forum to assess compliance and discuss treaty modifications.

Article X: Right of Withdrawal

- This provision allows a country to withdraw from the treaty if it determines that extraordinary circumstances have jeopardized its security.

- While the NPT remains in effect, it has faced challenges, including withdrawals. The most significant withdrawal occurred in 2003, when North Korea became the first state to exit the treaty, citing U.S. hostility. This led to its subsequent nuclear tests and development of nuclear weapons.

Treaty Effectiveness and Challenges

The United States and Russia (formerly the Soviet Union) have reduced their nuclear arsenals through treaties such as START (Strategic Arms Reduction Treaty), but complete disarmament remains elusive. Despite its success in curbing nuclear proliferation, the NPT has notable limitations:

- Lack of Disarmament Progress: While non-nuclear states are bound by strict non-proliferation rules, nuclear-armed states have not fully committed to disarmament, despite their obligations under Article VI.

- Non-Signatories Possessing Nuclear Weapons: Countries like India, Pakistan, and Israel have developed nuclear weapons without NPT membership, raising concerns about the treaty's ability to enforce global nuclear security.
- Verification Challenges: While the IAEA conducts inspections, clandestine nuclear programs can still exist, as seen in cases like North Korea and Iran.
- Withdrawal Loophole: Article X allows states to withdraw from the treaty if they deem their "supreme national interests" to be threatened. This provision was used by North Korea to exit the NPT and develop nuclear weapons.

Chapter Conclusion: NPT a Cornerstone of Global Nuclear Security

The Treaty on the Non-Proliferation of Nuclear Weapons (NPT) remains the cornerstone of global nuclear security. It has successfully limited nuclear proliferation yet struggles with enforcement and disarmament. While nuclear-armed states have reduced their arsenals, complete nuclear disarmament remains a distant goal. The challenge ahead is to strengthen verification mechanisms, push for universal adherence, and ensure that nuclear-weapon states honor their commitments under Article VI.

The NPT remains the most comprehensive and widely accepted framework for nuclear non-proliferation and disarmament, but its success depends on strict enforcement, international cooperation, and political will. While it has effectively limited nuclear proliferation, challenges such as non-compliance, slow disarmament progress, and geopolitical conflicts continue to threaten its objectives. Future negotiations and amendments will determine whether the treaty can adapt to modern nuclear challenges and uphold global security in the decades ahead.

Chapter (5)

The Strategic Arms Limitation Talks and the Anti-Ballistic Missile Treaty

"As nuclear weapons spread into more and more hands, the calculus of deterrence grows increasingly ephemeral and deterrence less and less reliable. In a widely proliferated world, it becomes ever more difficult to decide who is deterring whom and by what calculations"

Henry Kissinger

The mid-20th century was defined by the shadow of nuclear annihilation. The aftermath of World War II left the world divided between two superpowers—the United States and the Soviet Union—both locked in an arms race that seemed to have no end. The Cuban Missile Crisis of 1962 demonstrated just how close humanity had come to catastrophe, and from the rubble of that crisis emerged a growing realization: if neither side stepped back, nuclear warfare was inevitable.

This realization led to a series of negotiations and agreements, beginning with the establishment of the

International Atomic Energy Agency (IAEA) in 1957 to monitor nuclear activities. The Limited Test Ban Treaty (LTBT) of 1963 prohibited nuclear tests in the atmosphere, underwater, and in space, marking the first major step in arms control. Then came the Treaty on the Non-Proliferation of Nuclear Weapons (NPT) in 1968, which sought to prevent the spread of nuclear weapons beyond the five recognized nuclear states.

But limiting nuclear proliferation was not enough. The focus had to shift toward limiting the weapons themselves. This realization paved the way for the Strategic Arms Limitation Talks (SALT) and, eventually, the Anti-Ballistic Missile (ABM) Treaty—a monumental effort to curb the dangerous escalation of the nuclear arms race.

The SALT Negotiations: A Path to Arms Control

The Strategic Arms Limitation Talks (SALT I), held from November 17, 1969, to May 26, 1972, were groundbreaking negotiations between the United States and the Soviet Union at the height of the Cold War. The discussions sought to place mutual limits on nuclear arms, particularly the development of Intercontinental Ballistic Missiles (ICBMs), Submarine-Launched Ballistic Missiles (SLBMs), and Anti-Ballistic Missile (ABM) systems.

These negotiations were catalyzed by President Lyndon B. Johnson's 1967 realization that the Soviet Union had started constructing an ABM system around Moscow. The development of such a system could have upset the fragile balance of power, allowing the Soviets to launch a first strike and then neutralize any U.S. retaliation.

In 1967, Johnson met with **Soviet Premier Alexei Kosygin** at Glassboro State College, where Johnson stressed the need for arms control: *"We must gain control of the ABM race[40],"* Johnson urged, emphasizing that uncontrolled escalation could lead to an arms race with no winners.

Secretary of Defense **Robert McNamara**, who had long warned against the dangers of unchecked nuclear proliferation, called the arms race: *"An insane road to follow[41]"*.

Although the two leaders failed to reach a definitive agreement at Glassboro, Johnson's initiative laid the foundation for what would become SALT I.

The Negotiations: Challenges and Breakthroughs

The formal SALT talks began under President Richard Nixon in Helsinki in 1969. Over the next two and a half years, U.S. and Soviet delegations met in both Helsinki

---

[40] https://history.state.gov/milestones/1969-1976/salt
[41] https://history.state.gov/milestones/1969-1976/salt

and Vienna, struggling to reconcile their fundamental strategic differences.

The Soviet Union initially insisted on restricting negotiations to ABM systems, arguing that limitations on offensive nuclear weapons should be deferred. The U.S. delegation, led by Gerard Smith, opposed this view, arguing to limit ABM systems but allow unrestricted growth of offensive weapons would be incompatible with the basic objectives of SALT.

This impasse led to a deadlock that lasted more than a year. It was finally broken on May 20, 1971, when Washington and Moscow announced their common agreement:

- To negotiate a permanent treaty limiting ABM systems.

- To achieve certain limitations on offensive weapons, albeit on a temporary basis.

That was announced in a statement read by Richard M. Nixon (The US President) Washington 12 O'clock; Moscow 7 pm:

"The Governments of the United States and the Soviet Union, after reviewing the course of their talks on the limitation of strategic armaments, have agreed to concentrate this year on working out an agreement for the limitation of the deployment of anti-ballistic missile systems (ABMs). They have also agreed that, together with concluding an agreement to limit ABMs, they will agree on certain measures with respect to the limitation of offensive strategic weapons.

The two sides are taking this course in the conviction that it will create more favorable conditions for further negotiations to limit all strategic arms. These negotiations will be actively pursued. This agreement is a major step in breaking the stalemate on nuclear arms talks. Intensive negotiations, however, will be required to translate this understanding into a concrete agreement.

This statement that I have just read expresses the commitment of the Soviet and American Governments at the highest levels to achieve that goal. If we succeed, this joint statement that has been issued today may well be remembered as the beginning of a new era in which all nations will devote more of their energies and their resources not to the weapons of war, but to the works of peace"[42].

The Outcome: ABM Treaty and the Interim Agreement

After extensive deliberations, President Nixon and General Secretary Brezhnev met in Moscow on May 26, 1972, to finalize the first round of the SALT agreements. The two sides signed:

- **The Anti-Ballistic Missile (ABM) Treaty,** which limited each country to two ABM deployment areas (later reduced to one) and prohibited the development of a nationwide missile defense system.

---

[42] https://millercenter.org/the-presidency/presidential-speeches/may-20-1971-remarks-announcing-agreement-strategic-arms

- **The Interim Agreement on Strategic Offensive Arms**, a five-year freeze on the number of ICBMs and SLBMs each side could possess.

On October 3, 1973, in the East Room at the White House following the remarks of Andrei A. Gromyko, Soviet Minister of Foreign Affairs at the ceremony marking entry into force of the Treaty on the Limitation of Anti-Ballistic Missile Systems and the Interim Agreement on the Limitation of Strategic Offensive Arms, President Nixon remarked:

"I think all of us are quite aware of the fact that the signing of these documents today, the signing of the documents that occurred earlier this year in the Kremlin, raise the hopes of all the people of the world for a dream of mankind from the beginning of civilization, a world of peace, a world in which peoples with different governments and different philosophies could live in peace together. We believe that we have contributed to that cause and to the realization of that dream. And as we take this first step, we look forward to working together in taking the next steps, we look forward particularly in being worthy of the hopes of the people of the world. And we can be worthy of those hopes if our two great nations can move together, not only to limit the burden of arms on ourselves but to lift the burden of fear of war from all of the people of the world[43]".

Foreign Minister Gromyko spoke in Russian echoed this sentiment:

---

[43] https://www.presidency.ucsb.edu/documents/remarks-ceremony-marking-entry-into-force-the-treaty-the-limitation-anti-ballistic-missile

"The *treaty and the interim agreement on questions of strategic arms limitation, which were signed in Moscow by you, Mr. President, and by the General Secretary of the Central Committee of the Communist Party of the Soviet Union, Leonid Brezhnev, and which are today coming into force, will go down in history as a significant achievement in restraining the arms race.*

This is how the significance of this event is evaluated by world public opinion. The Soviet Union attaches great importance to these accords which are a continuation of the process initiated by the conclusion of the Moscow Test Ban Treaty, the Treaty on the Non-Proliferation of Nuclear Weapons, and other important agreements limiting the arms race in the world.........For the first time since the Second World War, agreements are coming into force aimed at slowing down the race in the most destructive types of armaments, but any treaty and any agreement can have a genuine historic significance only when the principles and the intentions proclaimed in them become the content of the practical activity of states and lead to further important achievements in that direction.[44]".

Verification and Compliance

One of the biggest challenges of the SALT agreements was verification. Both nations refused to allow on-site inspections, leading to the adoption of National Technical Means (NTM)—a system relying on satellites, radar tracking, and telemetry data to monitor compliance.

---

[44] https://www.presidency.ucsb.edu/documents/remarks-ceremony-marking-entry-into-force-the-treaty-the-limitation-anti-ballistic-missile

Both parties explicitly agreed not to interfere with each other's verification systems. Additionally, a Standing Consultative Commission (SCC) was created to address concerns and resolve disputes.

SALT I marked the first serious attempt at nuclear arms control between the Cold War adversaries. While it did not reduce the number of nuclear weapons, it stabilized the arms race and laid the groundwork for further negotiations, including SALT II and the later Strategic Arms Reduction Treaties (START).

The signing of SALT I was a defining moment in Cold War diplomacy, proving that even the world's most powerful adversaries could negotiate limits on the most dangerous weapons ever created.

The ABM Treaty: Objectives and Key Provisions

The Anti-Ballistic Missile (ABM) Treaty, signed on May 26, 1972, between the United States and the Soviet Union, was a landmark arms control agreement designed to limit missile defence systems in order to preserve the concept of Mutual Assured Destruction (MAD). The core objective was to prevent either side from developing a missile defence system that could encourage a first-strike capability, thus destabilizing the nuclear balance.

The agreement was unlimited in duration but allowed for withdrawal under specific conditions if one party determined that its "supreme national interests" were at risk.

The ABM Treaty imposed several strict limitations on missile defence systems to ensure neither side could develop an effective shield against nuclear attacks:

Article III: Limited ABM Deployment Areas

Each party could deploy one ABM site near its national capital and one near an ICBM launch site, with a maximum of 100 interceptor missiles at each location. This restriction ensured neither country could build a comprehensive missile defence system.

Article V: Ban on Sea-, Air-, Space-, and Mobile Land-Based ABM Systems

- The treaty strictly prohibited the development, testing, or deployment of ABM systems on ships, aircraft, in space, or as mobile land-based systems.
- This clause was crucial to prevent a technological arms race in missile defence capabilities.

Article VI: Restrictions on ABM Components

- The treaty forbade modifying existing radars, missiles, or launchers to function as ABM systems.
- Nations were only allowed to place early-warning radars along the periphery of their national territories, facing outward, to prevent their use as ABM radars.

Article VII: Modernization and Replacement Provisions

While ABM systems could not expand, both parties could modernize or replace their existing ABM components, provided they did not increase their effectiveness beyond the agreed limits.

Article VIII: Dismantling of Prohibited ABM Systems

Any ABM systems deployed beyond the treaty's constraints had to be dismantled within an agreed period.

Article IX: Non-Transfer Clause

The treaty explicitly forbade the transfer of ABM technology or components to third-party nations, ensuring the agreement remained exclusive to the U.S. and the USSR.

Article XII: Verification and Compliance

Each party agreed to use national technical means of verification, such as spy satellites, to monitor compliance. Both sides pledged not to interfere with the other's verification efforts or use deliberate concealment measures.

Article XIII: Standing Consultative Commission

A permanent U.S.-Soviet Commission was established to resolve disputes, discuss compliance issues, and oversee treaty implementation.

Article XV: Right to Withdraw

Either nation could withdraw if "extraordinary events related to the subject matter of the Treaty" jeopardized its supreme interests. A six-month notice period was required before withdrawal.

The Interim Agreement on the Limitation of Strategic Offensive Arms and Key Provisions

Alongside the ABM treaty, this interim agreement was signed off on May 26, 1972, between the United States and the Soviet Union for a period of 5 years. Key Clauses of the Interim Agreement are[45]:

Article I: ICBM Launcher Restrictions

Both parties agreed not to start construction of additional fixed land-based intercontinental ballistic missile (ICBM) launchers after July 1, 1972.

Article II: Conversion Prohibition

Neither party could convert older land-based ICBM launchers (deployed before 1964) into launchers for newer, heavy ICBMs.

Article III: SLBM (Submarine-Launched Ballistic Missile) Limits

The number of SLBM launchers and modern ballistic missile submarines was frozen at the levels operational and under construction as of the signing date. New SLBM launchers could only be deployed as replacements for

---

[45] Interim Agreement on certain measures with respect to the limi tation of strategic offensive arms (with protocol). Signed at Moscow on 26 May 1972 Authentic texts: English and Russian. Registered by the United States of America on 2 August 1974.

older ICBM launchers (pre-1964) or older submarine launchers.

Article IV: Modernization & Replacement

Allowed modernization and replacement of ballistic missiles and launchers, as long as it did not increase the total number of launchers.

Article V: Verification

- Each party would verify compliance through national technical means (satellite reconnaissance, etc.).
- Neither side would interfere with the other's verification efforts.
- Deliberate concealment measures that hinder verification were prohibited.

Article VI: Consultative Commission

Established the Standing Consultative Commission to oversee the agreement's implementation and compliance.

Article (VII): Commitment to Further Negotiations

The agreement did not prejudge future negotiations on additional limitations of strategic offensive arms.

Article (VIII): Duration & Withdrawal

- The agreement would remain in force for 5 years unless replaced by a new arms control agreement.

- Either party could withdraw with six months' notice if it determined that extraordinary circumstances jeopardized its security.

This agreement marked the first arms control agreement between the U.S. and USSR to limit strategic offensive weapons, though it was only a temporary measure intended to pave the way for further negotiations, leading to SALT II.

ABM Impact on Strategic Stability and Mutual Assured Destruction (MAD)

The ABM Treaty was rooted in the concept of Mutual Assured Destruction (MAD)—the principle that both sides would be deterred from nuclear war by the certainty of   retaliation.
By limiting missile defence, the treaty ensured that neither country could effectively prevent a counterattack, thereby maintaining nuclear deterrence.

During the negotiations, I imagine that both the U.S. National Security Advisor Henry Kissinger and the Soviet diplomat Viktor Karpov believed that it was paramount to maintain the balance of terror, as however grim, is going to be more stable than the illusion of invulnerability and uncertainty, i.e. If either side believes it can strike without consequences, the world will become massively more danger, which unfortunately is the world we are living in today.

The treaty did not limit offensive nuclear weapons, but its symbolic and strategic importance made it a pillar of Cold War arms control. The ABM Treaty of 1972 was a critical step in controlling the nuclear arms race by restricting defensive capabilities, thereby preserving deterrence. It was a testament to the idea that less defence could mean greater security in the nuclear age.

For nearly three decades, the treaty helped maintain strategic stability, but its relevance was later challenged by emerging missile threats and new U.S. defence doctrines, ultimately leading to its U.S. withdrawal in 2002.

The legacy of the ABM Treaty remains a key lesson in arms control diplomacy: that mutual vulnerability can, paradoxically, be a force for peace.

Tensions and Early Signs of Strain

Despite the treaty's **intentions**, both the U.S. and the Soviet Union occasionally pushed the limits of the agreement:

- **Soviet ABM Violations (1983-1986):** The U.S. accused the Soviet Union of violating the treaty by constructing a large radar system in Krasnoyarsk, Siberia, which the Reagan administration claimed could be used for missile defence rather than early warning (as required by the treaty). The Soviets eventually dismantled the radar after U.S. pressure

.

- **U.S. Strategic Defence Initiative (SDI) - "Star Wars" (1983):** President **Ronald Reagan** proposed a space-based missile defence system, prompting Soviet concerns that SDI violated the spirit, if not the letter, of the ABM Treaty. While SDI never materialized, it deepened distrust and led to heated arms control negotiations.

- **Post-Soviet Tensions (1990s):** After the collapse of the Soviet Union in 1991, Russia inherited the treaty obligations, but the U.S. increasingly questioned whether ABM limitations remained relevant in a world where the nuclear threat had evolved.

The U.S. Withdrawal (2001) and Rationale

By the late 1990s and early 2000s, the geopolitical landscape had changed dramatically. The U.S. was no longer facing a single strategic adversary in Russia but rather emerging threats from rogue states and non-state actors.

President George W. Bush, citing missile threats from nations like North Korea and Iran, argued that the ABM Treaty was outdated and no longer served U.S. security interests:

"I have concluded the ABM Treaty hinders our government's ability to develop ways to protect our people from future terrorist or rogue state missile attacks" ... "The 1972 ABM Treaty was signed... in a vastly different world. One of the signatories, the Soviet Union, no longer exists[46]"

The key **U.S. justifications** for withdrawing included:

- **Emerging Missile Threats:** The growing development of ballistic missile programs in North Korea, Iran, and Iraq prompted U.S. officials to reconsider missile defence.

- **Technological Advancements:** U.S. research into new missile defence technologies— particularly ground-based interceptors—was constrained by ABM Treaty restrictions.

- **Terrorism & Asymmetrical Warfare:** Following the 9/11 attacks, the Bush administration reevaluated national security priorities, shifting focus from Cold War-style deterrence to proactive defence strategies.

---

[46] https://www.armscontrol.org/act/2002-01/us-withdrawal-abm-treaty-president-bushs-remarks-and-us-diplomatic-notes

On December 13, 2001, the United States officially announced its withdrawal from the ABM Treaty, effective June 13, 2002, stating in a text of diplomatic notes to Russia, Belarus, Kazakhstan, and Ukraine:

"The Embassy of the United States of America has the honor to refer to the Treaty between the United States of America and the Union of Soviet Socialist Republics (USSR) on the Limitation of Anti-Ballistic Missile Systems signed at Moscow May 26, 1972.

Article XV, paragraph 2, gives each Party the right to withdraw from the Treaty if it decides that extraordinary events related to the subject matter of the treaty have jeopardized its supreme interests. The United States recognizes that the Treaty was entered into with the USSR, which ceased to exist in 1991. Since then, we have entered into a new strategic relationship with Russia that is cooperative rather than adversarial and are building strong relationships with most states of the former USSR.

Since the Treaty entered into force in 1972, a number of state and non-state entities have acquired or are actively seeking to acquire weapons of mass destruction. It is clear, and has recently been demonstrated, that some of these entities are prepared to employ these weapons against the United States. Moreover, a number of states are developing ballistic missiles, including long-range ballistic missiles, as a means of delivering weapons of mass destruction. These events pose a direct threat to the territory and security of the United States and jeopardize its supreme interests. As a result, the United States has concluded that it must develop, test, and deploy anti-ballistic missile systems for the defense of its national territory, of its forces outside the United States, and of its friends and allies.

Pursuant to Article XV, paragraph 2, the United States has decided that extraordinary events related to the subject matter of the Treaty have jeopardized its supreme interests. Therefore, in the exercise of the right to withdraw from the Treaty provided in Article XV, paragraph 2, the United States hereby gives notice of its withdrawal from the Treaty. In accordance with the terms of the Treaty, withdrawal will be effective six months from the date of this notice"[47].

Russian Response to U.S. Withdrawal

While Russia criticized the U.S. decision, it reacted cautiously at first. **President Vladimir Putin** stated: *"The U.S. withdrawal from the ABM Treaty is a mistake. However, this does not pose an immediate threat to Russia's security[48]." (December 2001).*

Initially, Russia sought diplomatic responses rather than an immediate countermeasure. However, the U.S. continued missile defence developments, including:

- Deploying Ground-Based Midcourse Defence (GMD) interceptors in Alaska and California.

- Expanding NATO missile defence **systems** in **Europe**, citing threats from Iran.

---

[47] Department of State - Text of Diplomatic Notes to Russia, Belarus, Kazakhstan, and Ukraine, December 13, 2001

[48] https://www.voanews.com/a/a-13-a-2001-12-13-12-putin-66405747/549270.html

By the late 2010s, Russia increasingly viewed these developments as a direct threat, leading to countermeasures.

Russia's 2020 Withdrawal and Justification

In response to continued U.S. advancements in missile defence, Russia formally withdrew from all remaining commitments to the ABM Treaty in 2020.

Russian officials cited the U.S. deployment of missile defence systems in Eastern Europe, particularly the Aegis Ashore systems in Romania and Poland, as evidence that the spirit of the treaty had already been abandoned.

Although Russia has conducted research on hypersonic weapons technology since the 1980s, its efforts were accelerated in response to U.S. missile defence deployments in both the United States and Europe, and to respond to the U.S. withdrawal from the ABM treaty. In that sentiment, President Putin stated that: *"the US is permitting constant, uncontrolled growth of the number of anti-ballistic missiles, improving their quality, and creating new missile launching areas. If we do not do something, eventually this will result in the complete devaluation of Russia's nuclear potential. Meaning that all of our missiles could simply be intercepted[49]".*

---

[49] Vladimir Putin, "Presidential Address to the Federal Assembly," March 1, 2018, at http://en.kremlin.ru/events/ president/news/56957

This seemed to be a retaliatory response to restore the strategic stability and the balance of terror against the US missile defences.

Geopolitical Impact of the ABM Treaty's Demise

The collapse of the ABM Treaty marked the beginning of a new arms race between global powers. Without treaty-imposed restrictions, the United States, Russia, and China began accelerating their missile defence and offensive capabilities, leading to unprecedented developments in strategic weapons.

A New Arms Race

The U.S. Expansion of Missile Defense Systems: Following its withdrawal, the United States significantly expanded its missile defense programs, including:

Ground-Based Midcourse Defence (GMD): Interceptor sites in Alaska and California to counter long-range missile threats.

Aegis Ballistic Missile Defence System: Expanded to European NATO allies, placing missile interceptors in Poland and Romania, which Russia viewed as a violation of previous arms control agreements.

Space-Based Infrared System (SBIRS): A satellite network designed to detect and track missile launches globally.

Russia's Development of Hypersonic Glide Vehicles (HGVs) and ICBMs:

After the U.S. withdrawal from the ABM Treaty in 2002, Russia announced the development of hypersonic weapons designed to evade missile defence systems. These included:

Avangard Hypersonic Glide Vehicle (HGV) – Capable of reaching speeds of **Mach 20**, making it nearly impossible to intercept.

RS-28 Sarmat ("Satan-2") ICBM – Designed to carry multiple nuclear warheads with an unpredictable flight path, bypassing U.S. missile defences.

Kinzhal Hypersonic Missile – Deployed with air-launched platforms, capable of hitting U.S. and NATO assets.

Breakdown of Arms Control Agreements

The ABM Treaty's collapse destabilized the international arms control framework, leading to the breakdown of other critical treaties:

The INF Treaty (1987-2019):

The Intermediate-Range Nuclear Forces (INF) Treaty was scrapped in 2019, with the U.S. citing Russian violations and Russia accusing the U.S. of expanding missile defence systems that could be converted into offensive weapons.

New START Uncertainty (2021-Present):

With no replacement agreements in place, the New START Treaty, set to expire in 2026, faces an uncertain future. Russia and the U.S. have accused each other of non-compliance, further weakening global arms control efforts.

The Militarization of Space:

With no ABM restrictions, both Russia and the U.S. began exploring space-based missile defence and offensive capabilities, including anti-satellite weapons.

NATO-Russia Tensions

The end of the ABM Treaty coincided with escalating tensions between Russia and NATO, particularly following Russia's 2014 annexation of Crimea:

Expansion of NATO Missile Defenses:

NATO deployed U.S. missile defense systems in Poland and Romania, citing threats from Iran. However, Russia viewed these deployments as a direct security threat, claiming that NATO's missile interceptors could be converted into offensive nuclear platforms.

Russia's Military Response:

- In 2016, Russia deployed **Iskander-M nuclear-capable missiles** in **Kaliningrad**, directly targeting NATO military infrastructure.
- Russian **military exercises along NATO borders** increased, with simulated nuclear strikes conducted in response to NATO's missile defense expansion.

2014 Crimea Crisis & Military Buildup:

Russia's annexation of **Crimea** and its military involvement in **Ukraine** further deteriorated **U.S.-Russia relations**, making arms control negotiations nearly impossible.

China's Expanding Nuclear Capabilities

The ABM Treaty never included China, but its demise directly impacted Chinese military strategy. Without missile defense restrictions, China accelerated nuclear expansion to counter U.S. and Russian missile defense systems.

China's Nuclear Arsenal Expansion:

- Since 2002, China tripled its nuclear warhead stockpile, aiming to reach 1,000 warheads by 2030

- China deployed Multiple Independently Targetable Reentry Vehicles (MIRVs) on its DF-41 ICBMs, similar to Russia's RS-28 Sarmat.

Hypersonic Missile Development:

In 2021, China successfully tested a hypersonic glide vehicle capable of evading U.S. missile defenses, raising concerns in Washington about a new strategic imbalance.

Expansion into the South China Sea:

China deployed missile defense and offensive missile systems on artificial islands, further complicating U.S.-China military tensions.

In summary, the collapse of the ABM Treaty led to a fundamental shift in global security, resulting in:

A Renewed Nuclear Arms Race – The U.S., Russia, and China have all expanded their nuclear and missile defense capabilities, pushing the world toward a multipolar arms race.

The Erosion of Arms Control Agreements – Treaties like the INF Treaty and New START have either collapsed or face an uncertain future.

Increased NATO-Russia Confrontation – The expansion of NATO missile defense systems and Russia's military responses have fueled a new Cold War dynamic.

China's Emergence as a Strategic Competitor – Without arms control agreements, China has significantly expanded its nuclear and missile capabilities, altering the balance of power.

As global tensions rise, arms control diplomacy is at its weakest point in decades. Whether future agreements can replace the ABM Treaty remains uncertain, but its legacy continues to shape modern strategic policies

The Legacy of the ABM Treaty

The withdrawal of both the United States (2001) and Russia (2020) from the ABM Treaty signaled the end of Cold War-era arms control.

- The treaty had successfully stabilized nuclear deterrence for nearly three decades, but post-Cold War security challenges **undermined its relevance**.

- The U.S. withdrawal was driven by emerging missile threats and technological advancements, while Russia's response evolved over time, culminating in its own exit in 2020.

Today, the world faces a more uncertain nuclear future, with advancing missile technologies, hypersonic weapons, and new arms races emerging in a multipolar world order. Whether future arms control agreements can replace the ABM Treaty remains an open question—but its impact on global security is undeniable.

The Genesis of SALT II

In the intricate dance of Cold War diplomacy, the **Strategic Arms Limitation Talks II (SALT II)** emerged as a testament to the persistent efforts of the United States and the Soviet Union to curb the escalating nuclear arms race. This narrative unfolds over a series of negotiations, political challenges, and the relentless pursuit of strategic stability.

Following the foundational **SALT I** agreements in the early 1970s, both superpowers recognized the necessity for a more comprehensive treaty to further limit their strategic offensive weapons. Negotiations for SALT II commenced in **1972**, aiming to build upon the interim measures established by its predecessor.

Crafting the Treaty

After seven years of meticulous negotiations, a landmark moment was reached on June 18, 1979, in Vienna. U.S. President **Jimmy Carter** and Soviet General Secretary **Leonid Brezhnev** convened to sign the SALT II treaty, symbolizing a mutual commitment to arms control. During the signing ceremony, President Carter reflected on the significance of the treaty, stating:

"In setting our hands to this treaty, we set our nations on a safer course. We've labored long to make SALT II a safe and useful chart toward the future[50]*."*

Core Provisions:

The SALT II treaty introduced several pivotal limitations:

Delivery Vehicle Caps: Both nations agreed to restrict their total number of strategic nuclear delivery vehicles— including intercontinental ballistic missiles (ICBMs), submarine-launched ballistic missiles (SLBMs), and heavy bombers—to **2,250**[51].

MIRV Constraints: The treaty imposed specific sub-limits on launchers equipped with Multiple Independently targetable Reentry Vehicles (MIRVs), capping them at

---

[50] https://www.presidency.ucsb.edu/documents/vienna-summit-meeting-remarks-president-brezhnev-and-president-carter-signing-the-treaty
[51] https://history.state.gov/milestones/1969-1976/salt

1,320, with no more than **820** allocated to MIRVed ICBMs.

Ban on New Missile Programs: To prevent qualitative arms advancements, the development of new land-based ballistic missile systems was prohibited, except for one new type of light ICBM per side[52].

Verification Mechanisms:

To ensure compliance, both parties agreed to utilize National Technical Means (NTM), such as satellite reconnaissance and electronic signal collection, underscoring a mutual trust in technological verification[53].

Obstacles to Ratification:

Despite the treaty's historic signing, its journey toward ratification faced significant hurdles:

Political Opposition: Within the United States, a coalition of Republicans and conservative Democrats expressed skepticism regarding the Soviet Union's adherence to the treaty and the sufficiency of its verification measures.

---

[52] https://atomicarchive.com/resources/treaties/salt-II.html
[53] https://history.state.gov/milestones/1969-1976/salt

Geopolitical Tensions: The Soviet invasion of Afghanistan in **December 1979** exacerbated global tensions. In response, President Carter requested the Senate to defer consideration of the treaty, leading to its eventual stagnation.

Legacy of SALT II:

Although never formally ratified, both superpowers initially pledged to honor the treaty's terms. This mutual understanding persisted until **1986**, when the United States accused the Soviet Union of violations, prompting a withdrawal from its obligations.

The SALT II negotiations and the resulting treaty, despite its challenges, laid critical groundwork for subsequent arms control agreements, such as the **Strategic Arms Reduction Treaty (START)**, marking a continued effort toward global strategic stability.

Chapter Conclusion: A Legacy of Unfinished Promises and Lingering Shadows

As the ink dried on the **Strategic Arms Limitation Talks (SALT)** and the **Anti-Ballistic Missile (ABM) Treaty**, the world stood at the precipice of an uncertain future. These agreements were not mere diplomatic formalities—they were desperate attempts to tame the nuclear behemoth that had loomed over humanity since the dawn of the Cold War.

The **SALT I accords** marked a significant step toward arms control, but they were far from a definitive solution. The **ABM Treaty**, in particular, sought to preserve the precarious balance of **Mutual Assured Destruction (MAD)** by preventing the development of defensive shields that could encourage a first-strike capability. However, in a world where mistrust reigned supreme, limiting one aspect of the arms race only fueled competition elsewhere.

It was a **fragile peace**, built not on trust, but on the unshakable certainty that both superpowers held the power to obliterate each other in a matter of minutes.

The **negotiations were arduous**, marked by moments of deadlock, compromise, and historic breakthroughs. Nixon and Brezhnev, standing at opposite ends of an ideological chasm, **signed their names in history**, not as allies, but as adversaries seeking survival. Their signatures symbolized a grudging acknowledgment that unchecked nuclear escalation was a game with no winners—only annihilation.

Yet, the **true measure of an arms control treaty is not found in its signing, but in its endurance**. SALT I provided **temporary relief**, a momentary pause in the relentless pursuit of military superiority. But it was just that—a pause. The world soon realized that freezing numbers did not erase the lurking dangers of nuclear conflict. The limitations were neither deep nor permanent, and the expiration of the **Interim Agreement** in 1977 left a void that SALT II struggled to fill.

As the years passed, **diplomatic idealism clashed with geopolitical reality**. The Soviet invasion of Afghanistan, the rise of new missile technologies, and a shifting global power structure eroded the very foundation on which these treaties were built. By the early 2000s, the **ABM Treaty was abandoned**, dismissed as an outdated relic of a bygone era. The very principles that once maintained global stability crumbled under the weight of new threats, new ambitions, and new fears.

Today, we stand in a world where the nuclear chessboard has grown infinitely more complex. The players have changed, the weapons have evolved, and the doctrines of deterrence have blurred into uncertainty. The collapse of these historic treaties did not bring peace—it **ushered in a new era of arms competition, an age of hypersonic missiles, cyber warfare, and strategic ambiguity**.

And so, we must ask ourselves: Was this the inevitable fate of arms control? Were the SALT negotiations and the ABM Treaty merely fleeting attempts to contain an arms race that was always destined to spiral out of control? Or do they still hold lessons for the future—a reminder that even in the darkest moments of human history, adversaries can choose dialogue over destruction?

The answer lies not in the treaties that were signed, nor in those that were abandoned. It lies in the choices we make now, in whether we learn from the past or repeat it. The story of **SALT and the ABM Treaty** is not just history—it is a warning. A warning that the pursuit of security through unchecked power is a dangerous illusion. A warning that no nation, no leader, and no ideology is immune to the consequences of a world where diplomacy is discarded, and deterrence is left to chance.

As the world races toward an uncertain future, one truth remains unchanged: **Arms control is not just an option—it is a necessity.** Whether we choose to heed that lesson will determine whether the next chapter in this story is one of peace—or of catastrophe.

Chapter (6)

The Intermediate-range Nuclear Forces (INF) Treaty & the Struggle for Hegemony between the U.S. and Russia

"The reward of a thing well done is to have done it"

Ralph Waldo Emerson

The Cold War was not just a battle of ideologies—it was a struggle for survival in an age of nuclear weapons. The world had never witnessed such a high-stakes rivalry between two superpowers, each armed with weapons capable of annihilating civilization. The United States and the Soviet Union, locked in an arms race, sought to outmatch each other at every turn, with nuclear arsenals expanding at an alarming rate. The pursuit of nuclear supremacy led to the development of intermediate-range nuclear missiles—capable of striking enemy targets in minutes—escalating global tensions to dangerous levels. The mere presence of these weapons was a threat to peace, bringing humanity to the brink of catastrophe.

Yet, within this perilous environment, diplomatic efforts emerged, not from idealism but from necessity. The fear of mutual destruction forced both sides to engage in arms control negotiations, setting the stage for one of the most pivotal treaties in Cold War history: the **Intermediate-Range Nuclear Forces (INF) Treaty**, signed in 1987. But to understand how the world arrived at that moment, one must look back at the steps taken—sometimes hesitantly, sometimes boldly—toward curbing nuclear proliferation.

The Foundations of Arms Control

Before the INF Treaty, there were attempts—however fragile—to establish frameworks for nuclear governance. The devastation of Hiroshima and Nagasaki had made one thing clear: nuclear weapons were not just powerful; they were a force beyond human control. The world needed safeguards, and so the journey toward arms control began.

The Birth of the IAEA (1957): Controlling the Nuclear Genie

In 1957, against the backdrop of a world divided by Cold War hostilities, an international effort was made to balance the **dual nature of nuclear technology**—its promise as an energy source and its peril as a weapon. The **International Atomic Energy Agency (IAEA)** was established under the United Nations, not as a disarmament agency but as a body ensuring that nuclear energy was used for peaceful purposes. The IAEA's role was pivotal in shaping the decades of arms control agreements that followed, serving as an early step in creating a structure of accountability between nuclear and non-nuclear states.

From Testing to Limiting Nuclear Arms

The 1960s saw the intensification of the arms race, but also the first real efforts to contain its environmental and human impact.

The Limited Test Ban Treaty (1963): A Step Toward Sanity

By the early 1960s, nuclear tests had become routine. Bombs were detonated in deserts, islands, and oceans, poisoning the environment with radioactive fallout. Scientists warned of the genetic consequences, and ordinary citizens feared the invisible dangers drifting through the atmosphere. The **Cuban Missile Crisis of 1962** had only deepened global anxieties, proving how close the world could come to an all-out nuclear exchange.

The response came in 1963 when the **United States, the Soviet Union, and the United Kingdom** signed the **Limited Test Ban Treaty (LTBT)**, prohibiting nuclear tests in the atmosphere, outer space, and underwater. Though it did not eliminate nuclear weapons, it was a symbolic and practical step toward reducing the reckless testing that had become commonplace.

The Nuclear Non-Proliferation Treaty (1968): Containing the Threat

While the LTBT addressed testing, the world still faced a growing problem: **nuclear proliferation**. More countries were seeking nuclear weapons, raising the terrifying prospect of a world where dozens of nations possessed the bomb.

To prevent this, the **Nuclear Non-Proliferation Treaty (NPT)** was signed in 1968, forging a critical agreement:

Nuclear-armed states (like the U.S. and USSR) pledged to work toward disarmament.

Non-nuclear states promised not to develop or acquire nuclear weapons.

The **IAEA** was given authority to verify compliance.

The NPT was far from perfect—many states accused nuclear powers of failing to uphold their end of the bargain—but it provided a crucial foundation for future arms control efforts.

The Strategic Arms Limitation Talks (SALT): Curbing the Arms Race

By the 1970s, both superpowers had built **massive** nuclear stockpiles, capable of destroying each other many times over. The realization that this race could not continue indefinitely led to the first direct attempts at limiting **strategic nuclear weapons**.

SALT I (1972): The First Real Breakthrough

Negotiated under **President Richard Nixon** and **Soviet Premier Leonid Brezhnev**, the **Strategic Arms Limitation Talks (SALT I)** resulted in two key agreements:

The Anti-Ballistic Missile (ABM) Treaty – This treaty limited the deployment of missile defense systems, ensuring that neither side could develop a shield to launch a first strike without fear of retaliation.

An Interim Agreement on Offensive Weapons – It froze the number of intercontinental ballistic missiles (ICBMs) and submarine-launched ballistic missiles (SLBMs) each side could have.

Though limited in scope, **SALT I** was a diplomatic breakthrough—it marked the first time the superpowers had agreed to restrain their nuclear competition.

SALT II (1979): A Treaty Undone by War

SALT I was followed by **SALT II**, which sought to put further caps on nuclear arsenals. Signed by **President**

Jimmy Carter and **Leonid Brezhnev**, it was a comprehensive agreement, but its fate was sealed when the Soviet Union **invaded Afghanistan in December 1979**. The U.S. Senate, unwilling to reward Soviet aggression, refused to ratify the treaty. Nevertheless, both sides largely followed its terms until the early 1980s.

The Road to the INF Treaty

Despite arms control efforts, the Cold War's nuclear tensions remained high. The late 1970s and early 1980s saw a new crisis emerge: the deployment of intermediate-range nuclear weapons in Europe.

The Soviet SS-20 Missile Crisis

In March 1976, the Soviet Union began deploying the SS-20 Saber (RSD-10 Pioneer), a mobile, intermediate-range ballistic missile equipped with three independently targetable nuclear warheads, each yielding 150 kilotons. With a range of approximately 4,700 to 5,000 kilometres, these missiles could strike targets across Western Europe, the Middle East, and parts of Asia from positions deep within Soviet territory. The SS-20's mobility and rapid launch capabilities made it difficult for NATO forces to track and counter, thereby shifting the strategic balance in Europe[54].

---

[54] https://missilethreat.csis.org/missile/ss-20-saber-rsd-10/

The introduction of the SS-20s was perceived by NATO as a significant escalation. Unlike their predecessors, the SS-4 and SS-5, which were less accurate and less mobile, the SS-20s presented a more versatile and survivable threat. This development prompted intense debates within NATO regarding appropriate countermeasures to restore the strategic equilibrium.

NATO's Dual-Track Decision (1979): Diplomacy and Deterrence

In response to the SS-20 deployment, NATO adopted the Dual-Track Decision on December 12, 1979. This strategy had two main components:

- **Diplomatic Track**: NATO sought arms control negotiations with the Soviet Union to limit intermediate-range nuclear forces, aiming for mutual restraint and reduction of such weapons.
- **Military Track**: Concurrently, NATO planned to deploy 108 Pershing II ballistic missiles and 464 ground-launched cruise missiles (GLCMs) in Western Europe by December 1983 if negotiations failed. This deployment was intended to counterbalance the SS-20 threat and maintain credible deterrence.

This dual approach was designed to pressure the Soviet Union into meaningful negotiations by demonstrating NATO's readiness to enhance its own capabilities while keeping the door open for diplomatic solutions. The decision underscored NATO's commitment to a balanced strategy of deterrence and dialogue.

The Zero-Option Proposal (1981): A Bold Offer

Upon taking office in 1981, U.S. President Ronald Reagan proposed the "Zero Option," a plan wherein the United States would cancel its deployment of Pershing II and GLCMs in Europe if the Soviet Union dismantled all its SS-20 missiles. This proposal aimed to eliminate an entire category of nuclear weapons from the European theatre.

However, the Soviet Union viewed this offer as one-sided, primarily because it did not account for British and French nuclear forces and thus rejected it. Consequently, negotiations stalled, and in 1983, the Soviets withdrew from the talks, leading to increased tensions and a subsequent military buildup in Europe.

Reagan and Gorbachev: A Turning Point (1985)

The impasse persisted until 1985, when Mikhail Gorbachev ascended to leadership in the Soviet Union. Recognizing the unsustainable nature of the arms race and the pressing need for economic and political reforms,

Gorbachev was open to reducing tensions with the West.

Gorbachev's approach marked a significant shift in Soviet policy, leading to a series of high-level meetings with President Reagan:

Geneva Summit (1985): Both leaders agreed that "a nuclear war cannot be won and must never be fought[55]," laying the groundwork for future arms control agreements.

Reykjavík Summit (1986): Although no agreement was reached, the discussions brought the two sides closer to understanding each other's positions on nuclear disarmament.

Washington Summit (1987): Culminating in the signing of the **Intermediate-Range Nuclear Forces (INF) Treaty** on December 8, 1987, The INF Treaty mandated the destruction of all U.S. and Soviet ground-launched ballistic and cruise missiles with ranges between 500 and 5,500 kilometres. By June 1, 1991, a total of 2,692 such missiles had been eliminated under strict verification protocols, marking a significant step toward de-escalation and the eventual end of the Cold War[56].

---

[55] https://www.theguardian.com/commentisfree/2024/dec/27/the-guardian-view-on-arms-control-essential-to-prevent-the-total-devastation-of-nuclear-war
[56] https://www.armscontrol.org/factsheets/intermediate-range-nuclear-forces-inf-treaty-glance

On December 8, 1987, President Ronal Reagon remarks on the ceremony of the INF treaty signing saying:

"This ceremony and the treaty we're signing today are both excellent examples of the rewards of patience. It was over 6 years ago, November 18, 1981, that I first proposed what would come to be called the zero option. It was a simple proposal -- one might say, disarmingly simple. Unlike treaties in the past, it didn't simply codify the status quo or a new arms buildup; it didn't simply talk of controlling an arms race.[57] "

"The numbers alone demonstrate the value of this agreement. On the Soviet side, over 1,500 deployed warheads will be removed, and all ground-launched intermediate-range missiles, including the SS - 20's, will be destroyed. On our side, our entire complement of Pershing II and ground-launched cruise missiles, with some 400 deployed warheads, will all be destroyed. Additional backup missiles on both sides will also be destroyed.[58]"

Gorbachev echoed this sentiment, stating that the treaty held is:

"The first-ever agreement eliminating nuclear weapons, has a universal significance for mankind, both from the standpoint of world politics and from the standpoint of humanism[59]."

---

[57] https://www.reaganlibrary.gov/archives/speech/remarks-signing-intermediate-range-nuclear-forces-treaty
[58] Remarks on Signing the Intermediate-Range Nuclear Forces Treaty | Ronald Reagan - https://www.reaganlibrary.gov/archives/speech/remarks-signing-intermediate-range-nuclear-forces-treaty
[59] https://www.reaganlibrary.gov/archives/speech/remarks-signing-intermediate-range-nuclear-forces-treaty

"The treaty offers a big chance at last to get onto the road leading away from the threat of catastrophe. It is our duty to take full advantage of that chance and move together toward a nuclear-free world, which holds out for our children and grandchildren and for their children and grandchildren the promise of a fulfilling and happy life without fear and without a senseless waste of resources on weapons of destruction[60]."

"We can be proud of planting this sapling, which may one day grow into a mighty tree of peace. But it is probably still too early to bestow laurels upon each other. As the great American poet and philosopher Ralph Waldo Emerson said: "The reward of a thing well done is to have done it.".[61]"

"May December 8, 1987, become a date that will be inscribed in the history books, a date that will mark the watershed separating the era of a mounting risk of nuclear war from the era of a demilitarization of human life[62]".

These developments marked a turning point in the Cold War, transitioning from confrontation to negotiation and setting the stage for the eventual end of the decades-long geopolitical standoff.

---

[60] https://www.reaganlibrary.gov/archives/speech/remarks-signing-intermediate-range-nuclear-forces-treaty

[61] https://www.reaganlibrary.gov/archives/speech/remarks-signing-intermediate-range-nuclear-forces-treaty

[62] https://www.reaganlibrary.gov/archives/speech/remarks-signing-intermediate-range-nuclear-forces-treaty

Purpose, Objectives and Key Elements of the INF Treaty

The Intermediate-Range Nuclear Forces (INF) Treaty, signed on December 8, 1987, was the first arms control agreement between the United States and the Soviet Union that aimed to eliminate an entire category of nuclear weapons rather than simply limit their numbers. Below are the key elements of the treaty, including the specific articles and clauses that define its obligations.

Article II & Article III: Weapons Covered

The treaty applied specifically to **ground-launched intermediate-range and shorter-range missiles**, as defined in **Article II**:

- **Intermediate-range missiles**: Missiles with a range **between 1,000 and 5,500 km** (Article II, Clause 5).

- **Shorter-range missiles**: Missiles with a range **between 500 and 1,000 km** (Article II, Clause 6).

Existing missile types covered under the treaty (Article III):

- **United States**: Pershing II ballistic missiles, BGM-109G cruise missiles.

- **Soviet Union**: SS-20, SS-4, SS-5 ballistic missiles, SSC-X-4 cruise missiles.

The treaty required both sides to eliminate all missiles of these types, including their launchers and associated support structures.

Article XI, Article XII, & Article XIII: Verification and Compliance

To ensure compliance, the treaty established one of the most comprehensive verification regimes in arms control history. These provisions are found in Articles XI, XII, and XIII.

On-Site Inspections (Article XI)

- Both sides agreed to allow **baseline inspections** to verify the number and location of missiles before elimination.

- **Closeout inspections** were conducted at facilities after missiles were removed.

- **Elimination inspections** confirmed the physical destruction of missiles and launchers.

- **Short-notice inspections** could be conducted at **any declared facility** to ensure compliance.

Exchange of Data (Article IX)

- Each side was required to **submit detailed reports** on the number, locations, and types of missiles, launchers, and support equipment they possessed.

- The data was **updated every six months** to track the progress of elimination.

Continuous Monitoring (Article XII)

- The treaty granted the **United States the right to monitor** the Soviet missile production facility at **Votkinsk.**

- The **Soviets were allowed to monitor** the U.S. facility at **Magna, Utah.**

- This was the **first** treaty to allow **permanent on-site inspections** at missile production sites.

Article XIII: Special Verification Commission (SVC)

The SVC was created as a dispute resolution mechanism to handle compliance issues and interpretations of the treaty. The Nuclear Risk Reduction Centers (NRRCs) were used to exchange notifications and communicate compliance concerns.

Article IV & Article V: Timetable for Elimination

The treaty set strict deadlines for the elimination of all intermediate-range and shorter-range missiles within three years of its entry into force (by June 1, 1991).

- **Initial reductions** had to begin immediately after the treaty entered into force.

- **By the end of 29 months** (May 1990), each side was required to have destroyed **at least half of its total declared missiles**.

- **By the end of three years** (June 1, 1991), all covered missile systems had to be **completely eliminated**.

Article X : Elimination Procedures

- Missiles were either dismantled, destroyed, or launched to destruction under the supervision of inspectors.

- Launchers, support structures, and equipment were dismantled in accordance with specific protocols outlined in the treaty.

Effectiveness of the Treaty, Breaches, Non-Compliance, and Withdrawal

The INF Treaty was one of the most successful arms control agreements of the Cold War era, leading to the verified elimination of 2,692 missiles. It marked the first time the United States and the Soviet Union agreed to eliminate an entire class of nuclear weapons rather than merely capping their numbers. The treaty not only removed thousands of nuclear warheads from global arsenals but also reduced tensions between the two superpowers, laying the groundwork for future arms reduction agreements such as START I (1991).

Success of the INF Treaty

The treaty was a landmark achievement in arms control and had a **significant impact on global security**:

2,692 nuclear missiles were dismantled and destroyed in accordance with treaty provisions.

- United States: Eliminated 846 missiles, including Pershing II ballistic missiles and BGM-109G ground-launched cruise missiles (GLCMs).
- Soviet Union: Destroyed 1,846 missiles, including SS-20, SS-4, SS-5, and SS-23 systems.

The treaty helped defuse Cold War tensions, leading to a new era of diplomatic engagement between Washington and Moscow.

It created one of the most rigorous verification regimes ever implemented, including on-site inspections and continuous monitoring at missile production sites in both countries.

The INF Treaty paved the way for further arms control agreements, including START I (1991), START II (1993), and New START (2010).

Allegations of Violations and Non-Compliance

Despite its initial success, mutual accusations of violations eventually undermined the treaty's integrity, leading to its collapse.

Russian Allegations of U.S. Violations

Russia has claimed that the U.S. deployment of Aegis Ashore systems in Eastern Europe, specifically in Romania (2016) and Poland (2022), could potentially violate the INF Treaty. The contention is that these systems, equipped with Mk-41 vertical launching systems, might be repurposed to launch offensive Tomahawk cruise missiles, which were prohibited under the treaty.

In his 2018 Presidential Address to the Federal Assembly, President Putin expressed significant concern over the U.S. intentions regarding the INF Treaty, stating: "*The unilateral withdrawal of the USA from the INF Treaty is the most urgent and most discussed issue in Russian American relations*[63]."

Additionally, during the Defence Ministry Board meeting on December 18, 2018, President Putin highlighted the potential threats posed by U.S. actions: "*The US leadership's statements about withdrawing from the INF Treaty are a source of major concern for us*[64]."

---

[63] https://www.en.kremlin.ru/events/president/transcripts/59863
[64] https://en.kremlin.ru/events/president/news/59431

U.S. Allegations of Russian Violations

The United States accused Russia of violating the treaty by developing and deploying the 9M729 (NATO designation: SSC-8) ground-launched cruise missile, which allegedly exceeded the 500–5,500 km range limit set by the INF Treaty.

In 2014, U.S. officials under President Barack Obama first raised concerns about the 9M729 missile, warning that it could undermine European security.

By 2017, under the Trump administration, the U.S. publicly declared Russia in "material breach" of the treaty.

In 2018, NATO issued a joint statement confirming Russia's violation and urging Moscow to return to compliance[65]:

" The Intermediate-Range Nuclear Forces (INF) Treaty has been crucial in upholding NATO's security for over 30 years.

Allies have concluded that Russia has developed and fielded a missile system, the 9M729, which violates the INF Treaty and poses significant risks to Euro-Atlantic security. We strongly support the finding of the United States that Russia is in material breach of its obligations under the INF Treaty.

We call on Russia to return urgently to full and verifiable compliance. It is now up to Russia to preserve the INF Treaty".

---

[65] https://www.nato.int/cps/en/natohq/official_texts_161122.htm

Former U.S. Secretary of State Mike Pompeo on February 2, 2019, in a press statement stated:

" The United States has concluded that extraordinary events related to the subject matter of the Treaty arising from Russia's continued noncompliance have jeopardized the United States' supreme interests, and the United States can no longer be restricted by the Treaty while Russia openly violates it. If Russia does not return to full and verifiable compliance with the Treaty by eliminating all 9M729 missiles, their launchers, and associated equipment in this six-month period, the Treaty will terminate[66].

Withdrawal from the Treaty

After years of rising tensions and accusations, the INF Treaty formally collapsed in 2019.

United States Withdrawal

On February 1, 2019, Donald Trump announced that his administration will officially suspend of U.S. obligations under the INF Treaty on 2nd February 2019, citing Russian non-compliance as the primary reason. Former U.S. President Donald Trump stated:

" The United States has fully adhered to the INF Treaty for more than 30 years, but we will not remain constrained by its terms while Russia misrepresents its actions. We cannot be the only country in the world unilaterally bound by this treaty, or any other. We will move forward with developing our own military response options and

---

[66] https://2017-2021.state.gov/u-s-intent-to-withdraw-from-the-inf-treaty-february-2-2019/

will work with NATO *and our other allies and partners to deny Russia any military advantage from its unlawful conduct"... "We stand ready to engage with Russia on arms control negotiations that meet these criteria, and, importantly, once that is done, develop, perhaps for the first time ever, an outstanding relationship on economic, trade, political, and military levels. This would be a fantastic thing for Russia and the United States, and would also be great for the world"[67].*

Russian Response

On February 2, 2019, following the United States' announcement to suspend its obligations under the Intermediate-Range Nuclear Forces (INF) Treaty, President Vladimir Putin declared that Russia would also suspend its participation. He stated:

"Our American partners have announced that they are suspending their participation in the treaty, and we are suspending it as well[68]."

Subsequently, on August 5, 2019, Russia formally withdrew from the INF Treaty, marking its official end after 32 years. President Putin remarked:

" It is with regret that Russia states that the unilateral withdrawal by the United States from the Treaty on the Elimination of Intermediate-Range and Shorter-Range Missiles under a far-fetched pretext and the dismantlement of one of the last fundamental arms

---

[67] https://trumpwhitehouse.archives.gov/briefings-statements/statement-president-regarding-intermediate-range-nuclear-forces-inf-treaty/
[68] https://en.kremlin.ru/events/president/news/59455/print

control treaties creates major complications for world affairs and brings about serious risks for everyone......... In this context, considering the current situation, I instruct the Defence Ministry, the Foreign Ministry and the Foreign Intelligence Service to monitor in the most thorough manner future steps taken by the United States to develop, produce and deploy intermediate-range and medium-range missiles....... If Russia obtains reliable information whereby the United States completes the development of these systems and starts to produce them, Russia will have no option other than to engage in a full-scale effort to develop similar missiles.......At the same time, Russia maintains the unilateral commitments it has assumed, and will act only when it has to respond,......... This scenario could signal a new start for an unfettered arms race. In order to avoid chaos with no rules, restrictions or laws, we need to once more weigh up all the dangerous consequences and launch a serious and meaningful dialogue free from any ambiguity[69]"

These developments underscore the reciprocal actions taken by both nations, leading to the dissolution of a pivotal arms control agreement.

The Legacy and Consequences of the INF Treaty's Collapse

The withdrawal of both the U.S. and Russia from the INF Treaty had profound implications for global security:

---

[69] https://washington.mid.ru/en/press-centre/news/statement_by_the_president_of_russia_on_the_unilateral_withdrawal_of_the_united_states_from_the_trea/

Return to an Arms Race

- With the INF Treaty gone, both the United States and Russia have resumed developing and testing intermediate-range missiles.
- In August 2019, just weeks after the treaty's expiration, the U.S. conducted a missile test previously banned under the INF Treaty.
- In 2020, Russia announced plans to deploy new intermediate-range weapons.

Increased NATO-Russia Tensions

- NATO allies expressed concern over Russia's deployment of 9M729 missiles in Europe.
- The U.S. has since explored stationing new missile systems in Europe and Asia—raising fears of a new Cold War-style standoff.

Impact on Other Arms Control Agreements

- The collapse of the INF Treaty weakened confidence in arms control diplomacy.
- The START (Strategic Arms Reduction Treaty) framework has faced challenges, as both Washington and Moscow increasingly distrust each other's commitment to arms control.

Chapter Conclusion: The INF Treaty and the Enduring Struggle for Hegemony

The Intermediate-Range Nuclear Forces (INF) Treaty was more than just a Cold War arms control agreement— it was a rare and significant diplomatic success that demonstrated the possibility of de-escalation in an era defined by nuclear rivalry. For more than three decades, the treaty helped curb the proliferation of intermediate-range nuclear weapons, reduced tensions between the United States and the Soviet Union (later Russia) and set a precedent for future arms control agreements.

At its core, the INF Treaty was a testament to the power of diplomacy amid geopolitical conflict. It showed that even at the height of a global ideological struggle, pragmatism and negotiation could prevail over brinkmanship and arms races. The agreement resulted in the destruction of 2,692 nuclear missiles, bolstered trust-building measures between Washington and Moscow, and set the stage for subsequent treaties like START I (1991) and New START (2010).

Yet, despite its early success, the treaty ultimately fell victim to the very dynamics it sought to restrain. As relations between the United States and Russia deteriorated in the post-Cold War world, mutual accusations of non-compliance, strategic mistrust, and shifting global security concerns led to the treaty's collapse. By August 2, 2019, after 32 years, both nations had formally withdrawn from the agreement, marking a return to an era of uncertainty in arms control.

A Treaty Undone by Hegemonic Rivalry

The demise of the INF Treaty underscores a harsh reality: as long as nuclear weapons remain instruments of power, arms control agreements will always be fragile, susceptible to shifts in geopolitical competition. The U.S. and Russia's decision to abandon the treaty was not merely a legal or technical matter—it reflected their broader strategic calculations in an evolving international landscape.

For the United States, the treaty was seen as a limitation on its ability to counter emerging threats, particularly from China, which was not bound by the INF Treaty and had built a formidable arsenal of intermediate-range missiles. For Russia, U.S. missile defence installations in Eastern Europe and NATO's expansion were perceived as direct threats, justifying Moscow's development of the 9M729 missile system, which Washington deemed a treaty violation.

These developments highlight a broader shift in global power dynamics—where the constraints of Cold War-era agreements are increasingly seen as incompatible with modern strategic realities.

The New Arms Race and Its Risks

With the collapse of the INF Treaty, the world now faces the renewed risk of an unfettered arms race. The United States and Russia have already begun testing and developing new missile systems, with both sides laying the groundwork for potential deployments in Europe and Asia. China, which was never part of the treaty, has continued expanding its intermediate-range missile capabilities, further complicating the global security equation.

The end of the INF Treaty also casts doubt on the future of other arms control agreements. The New START Treaty, the last remaining nuclear limitation agreement between the U.S. and Russia, has already faced renewed challenges and may also expire without renewal. Without new agreements or diplomatic efforts, the world risks entering a dangerous period of strategic instability—where the absence of legally binding treaties leads to greater uncertainty, miscalculations, and increased risks of escalation.

The INF Treaty's Enduring Legacy

Despite its dissolution, the INF Treaty remains a historic milestone in arms control. It demonstrated that disarmament was possible, proving that nations locked in a fierce power struggle could still find common ground in the pursuit of stability. The treaty's verification measures, and diplomatic framework set a standard for future arms reduction agreements, even as tensions between global powers continue to fluctuate.

The key lesson from the INF Treaty is that arms control agreements are only as strong as the political will behind them. The treaty's downfall was not due to its design but rather the strategic ambitions of its signatories. If arms control is to survive in the 21st century, new frameworks must be created that reflect the current multipolar world, involving not just the U.S. and Russia but also China, Europe, and other rising military powers.

In the end, the struggle for hegemony between the United States and Russia remains an unfinished story. The INF Treaty was a victory for diplomacy, but its demise is a warning about the fragility of international security. As the world moves forward, leaders must decide whether they will repeat the mistakes of the past or forge new pathways toward global stability. The choice, as history has shown, will shape the future of nuclear security and peace for generations to come.

Chapter (7)

The Strategic Arms Reduction Treaty (START) – Foundations of Nuclear Restraint in a Bipolar World

"It is an event of global significance, for we are imparting to the dismantling of the infrastructure of fear that has ruled the world, a momentum which is so powerful that it will be hard to stop"

Michail Gorbachev (President of the Soviet Union)

In the twilight of the Cold War, a quiet but dramatic race was nearing its end — not the race to the Moon or to military supremacy, but to survival itself.

It was the late 1980s. The world stood on a precarious edge, still haunted by the mushroom clouds of Hiroshima and Nagasaki. For decades, the United States and the Soviet Union had stockpiled weapons capable of ending civilization many times over. The nuclear arms race had become less a strategic contest and more a chilling ritual of mutual destruction. Each side watched the other through the crosshairs of ICBMs buried deep in concrete silos and lurking beneath the ocean in submarine-launched missiles.

But by the time Ronald Reagan and Mikhail Gorbachev met at Reykjavik in 1986, the world had begun to shift.

A Cold War Thaw — The Reagan-Gorbachev Gamble

Delving into the depth of the Reykjavik File - *Previously Secret U.S. and Soviet Documents on the 1986 Reagan-Gorbachev Summit*- reveals that in Reykjavik, the two leaders stunned their advisors by nearly agreeing to abolish nuclear weapons entirely. Though the talks collapsed over U.S. plans for a missile defense system — the infamous "Star Wars" Strategic Defense Initiative — the seed of arms control was planted deeper than ever before.

The Dream of Total Nuclear Abolition

Gorbachev came to Reykjavik prepared to pursue the "total liquidation of nuclear weapons based on the Soviet 15 January 1986 Program of Liquidation of Nuclear Weapons by the Year 2000". This goal was based on a Soviet initiative from January 15, 1986. His team was instructed to aim for a "breakthrough potential", emphasizing strategic weapons over nuclear testing[70]. In the evening Gorbachev gives additional instructions to Chernyaev on human rights and on the matter of

---

[70] https://nsarchive2.gwu.edu/NSAEBB/NSAEBB203/

Gorbachev's wife, Raisa Maksimovna, accompanying him to Iceland. "Gorbachev's ultimate goal for Reykjavik... is total liquidation of nuclear weapons... He reiterates it several times...[71]"

Reagan's Emphasis on SDI (Star Wars)

Reagan refused to abandon or limit SDI — the Strategic Defense Initiative. He saw it as a protective measure for a post-nuclear world, repeatedly using the "gas mask" analogy: just as one wouldn't discard gas masks after banning chemical weapons, SDI was needed as insurance[72]. Reagan: "Even if we eliminated all nuclear weapons, wouldn't we want to have protection against a madman with one missile?"

Gorbachev, however, viewed SDI as a first-strike enabler, fearing it would shift the arms race into space.

Soviet Misinterpretation and Mistrust

Source: Document 17 – *Negotiations by military experts (Akhromeev–Nitze), 11–12 Oct 1986*

This document, prepared as a result of the all-night discussion, outlined the disagreements but failed to

---

[71] Reykjavik File - Previously Secret U.S. and Soviet Documents on the 1986 Reagan-Gorbachev Summit-Document 5 – Gorbachev's instructions to Reykjavik prep group, October 4, 1986

[72] Reykjavik File - Previously Secret U.S. and Soviet Documents on the 1986 Reagan-Gorbachev Summit-Document 13 – U.S. Memorandum of Conversation, 12 October 1986 (3rd Meeting)

integrate the understandings achieved by the two leaders on October 11 or approached again on October 1 1986[73]

Soviet official Georgy Arbatov directly told U.S. negotiator Paul Nitze: *"What you are offering requires an exceptional level of trust. We cannot accept your position."* This quote underscored the deep **strategic distrust**, especially regarding American intentions with SDI.

Both Leaders Were Emotionally Invested

As the summit collapsed, Reagan pleaded personally for Gorbachev to agree to the deal. According to the **Soviet transcript**, Reagan said: *"I think you didn't want to achieve an agreement anyway... I don't know when we'll ever have another chance like this[74]."*

This emotional appeal was **absent in the U.S. transcript**, making the Soviet version especially revealing about Reagan's disappointment and belief that history was being lost.

This exchange comes after Reagan asks for a personal "favor" from Gorbachev of accepting the offer on SDI and ABM, and Gorbachev replies by saying this is not a favor but a matter of principle[75].

---

[73] https://nsarchive2.gwu.edu/NSAEBB/NSAEBB203/
[74] Reykjavik File - Previously Secret U.S. and Soviet Documents on the 1986 Reagan-Gorbachev Summit-Document 16 – Russian Transcript of Final Session, 12 Oct 1986

[75] https://nsarchive2.gwu.edu/NSAEBB/NSAEBB203/

Misaligned Expectations and Missed Opportunities

Shultz and the U.S. team **underestimated** Gorbachev's ambition. They expected a quiet prelude to a bigger summit, not dramatic proposals for 50% reductions and complete nuclear disarmament.

"We do not expect that Reykjavik will be a Summit... emphasis should be on preparation for a later one[76]."

This mismatch in expectations meant U.S. negotiators were caught off guard when Gorbachev came with sweeping disarmament ideas.

Gorbachev's Optimism After the Summit

Despite the summit's failure, Gorbachev remained hopeful:

"I am now even more of an optimist after Reykjavik... Reykjavik signifies a new stage in the process of disarmament — from limitations to total abolition[77]."

Internal Resistance from U.S. Military

While Reagan publicly supported elimination of ballistic missiles, **NSDD 250** walked back many radical ideas due to Pentagon resistance. The Joint Chiefs estimated that

---

[76] Reykjavik File - Previously Secret U.S. and Soviet Documents on the 1986 Reagan-Gorbachev Summit-Document 4 – Memo to Reagan from Secretary George Shultz, October 2, 1986

[77] Reykjavik File - Previously Secret U.S. and Soviet Documents on the 1986 Reagan-Gorbachev Summit-Document 19 – Gorbachev's reflections on the flight back to Moscow, 12 Oct 1986

abolishing missiles would require a massive increase in conventional forces.

"The Joint Chiefs promptly weighed in... that eliminating missiles would require large increases in conventional spending[78]."

Cold Realpolitik Returns Post-Summit

After Reykjavik, Gorbachev noted rising opposition to disarmament within the Soviet military, even as he sensed U.S. backtracking due to Iran-Contra.

"Americans are not doing anything in the spirit of Reykjavik... the generals here are hissing among themselves[79]."

The Reykjavik Summit documents reveal how remarkably close the U.S. and USSR came to ending the nuclear arms race — and how deep-rooted mistrust, political constraints, and institutional resistance derailed one of the most significant disarmament opportunities in history.

The Collapse in Slow Motion — Pressure Builds

By 1990, the Berlin Wall had fallen. Eastern European satellite states were shaking off their Soviet chains. German reunification loomed. The Warsaw Pact was

---

[78] Reykjavik File - Previously Secret U.S. and Soviet Documents on the 1986 Reagan-Gorbachev Summit-Document 25 – National Security Decision Directive 250, November 3, 1986

[79] Reykjavik File - Previously Secret U.S. and Soviet Documents on the 1986 Reagan-Gorbachev Summit-Document 28 – Gorbachev's Politburo Conference, December 1, 1986

crumbling. And in the heart of Moscow, the once ironclad grip of the Communist Party had begun to loosen.

The Soviet Union, still armed to the teeth, was beginning to dissolve — both politically and economically. Gorbachev, walking a geopolitical tightrope, believed the START Treaty would not only reduce tensions with the West but also offer a narrative of cooperation in an era of chaos.

At the Washington Summit in June 1990, U.S. President George H. W. Bush and Soviet President Mikhail Gorbachev issued a landmark Joint Statement to guide the next phase of arms control following the anticipated signing of the START Treaty.

The statement laid out a vision for enhancing strategic stability through deeper reductions and more cooperative frameworks, and it established principles that would echo directly in the START preamble. The Joint Statement highlighted the foundations for the next stage of the negotiations.

Presidents George H. W. Bush and Mikhail Gorbachev affirmed their commitment to completing the START Treaty, expressing *"satisfaction with the great progress"* and the aim to sign it by the end of 1990.

"They reaffirmed their determination to have the Treaty completed and ready for signature by the end of this year[80]."

They described START as a *"major landmark in both arms control and in the relationship[81]"* between the two superpowers.

The statement closed by affirming that the treaty fulfilled the Malta Summit objective and set the stage for deeper arms control: *"The two Presidents express confidence that the Foreign Ministers and the delegations… will be able to reach agreement in the remaining months on the outstanding issues that are still being negotiated[82]."*

The Signing Ceremony – A Moment of History

On **July 31, 1991**, beneath the ornate ceilings of the Kremlin's St. George Hall, President George H. W. Bush and President Mikhail Gorbachev signed the **START Treaty**. With the stroke of a pen, the two most dangerous arsenals on Earth had agreed to reduce their stockpiles and begin dismantling the architecture of Armageddon.

Gorbachev, facing growing domestic turmoil, called START a victory for reason:

---

[80] Soviet-United States Joint Statement on the Treaty on Strategic Offensive Arms | The American Presidency Project - https://www.presidency.ucsb.edu/documents/soviet-united-states-joint-statement-the-treaty-strategic-offensive-arms

[81] https://www.presidency.ucsb.edu/documents/soviet-united-states-joint-statement-the-treaty-strategic-offensive-arms

[82] https://www.presidency.ucsb.edu/documents/soviet-united-states-joint-statement-the-treaty-strategic-offensive-arms

"This is also a beginning -- the beginning of voluntary reduction of the nuclear arsenals of the U.S.S.R. and the United States, a process with unprecedented scope and objectives. It is an event of global significance, for we are imparting to the dismantling of the infrastructure of fear that has ruled the world, a momentum which is so powerful that it will be hard to stop....... It is important that there is a growing realization of the absurdity of overarmament now that the world has started to move toward an era of economic interdependence, and that the information revolution is making the indivisibility of the world ever more evident..... The document before us marks a moral achievement major breakthrough in our country's thinking and behavior. Our next goal is to make full use of this breakthrough to make disarmament an irreversible process[83]"

Bush, speaking with measured optimism, declared:

"The treaty that we sign today is a most complicated one -- the most complicated of contracts governing the most serious of concerns..... The START treaty vindicates an approach to arms control that guided us for almost a decade: the belief that we could do more than merely halt the growth of our nuclear arsenals. We could seek more than limits on the number of arms. In our talks we sought stabilizing reductions in our strategic arsenals. START makes that a reality. ...... The agreement itself is exceedingly complex, but the central idea at the heart of this treaty can be put simply: Stabilizing reductions in our strategic nuclear forces reduce the risk of war.... Neither side won unilateral advantage over the other... we take a significant step forward in dispelling a half-century of

[83] https://www.presidency.ucsb.edu/documents/remarks-president-gorbachev-and-president-bush-the-signing-ceremony-for-the-strategic-arms

mistrust......By reducing arms, we reverse a half-century of steadily growing strategic arsenals. But more than that, we take a significant step forward in dispelling a half-century of mistrust. By building trust, we pave a path to peace[84]."

It was a diplomatic triumph — yet bittersweet. Unknown to many watching, just five months later, the Soviet Union would cease to exist. The country that had signed the treaty no longer stood. Russia, inheriting the Soviet nuclear arsenal, would assume the treaty obligations.

Behind the Scenes: Tensions and Triumphs

The START Treaty was a compromise forged from realpolitik and necessity. It avoided addressing several controversial systems — such as **forward-deployed U.S. aircraft in Europe** or **sea-launched cruise missiles**, which the Soviets had tried to include. The Americans, for their part, secured verification measures for **mobile ICBMs**, which they feared were nearly impossible to track.

The U.S. emphasized verifiability — insisting, for instance, that launch canisters be distinguishable by type, and that mobile missiles be limited and tracked. The Soviets, cautious about exposure, sought to preserve strategic ambiguity but eventually accepted intrusive

---

[84] https://www.presidency.ucsb.edu/documents/remarks-president-gorbachev-and-president-bush-the-signing-ceremony-for-the-strategic-arms

inspections and agreed to exhibit sensitive systems like the Bear D bomber and heavy ICBMs.

Purpose and Objective of the Agreement

From 1982 to 1991, thousands of hours of negotiations took place in Geneva, Moscow, and Washington. The resulting document was unprecedented in scale and complexity. It wasn't just a treaty — it was a regulatory ecosystem, with over a dozen annexes, protocols, memorandums, and associated agreements.

The START Treaty sought to reduce and limit the two sides' strategic offensive arms. At its core, the treaty was an attempt to cap the nuclear arms race and prevent further escalation. The preamble reflects this intent:

START's central goals were:

- Reduce deployed strategic nuclear delivery vehicles (ICBMs, SLBMs, and heavy bombers).

- Cut the number of warheads to 6,000 each.

- Limit the throw-weight (total missile carrying capacity) of each side.

Even technical disagreements — such as whether a missile launch canister was part of the missile (the Soviets said yes; the U.S. insisted no) — were captured in protocols and resolved through Joint Compliance and Inspection Commission sessions.

The agreement embodied the Cold War-era principle of *strategic stability* — reducing the likelihood of a first-strike advantage while maintaining deterrence.

Key Provisions and Structure of the Treaty

The **Strategic Arms Reduction Treaty (START I)**, signed on **July 31, 1991**, was a monumental achievement in nuclear arms control. Its scope was vast, its mechanisms were unprecedented, and its legal structure was intricate and highly detailed. It aimed not only to reduce strategic nuclear weapons but also to establish a system of verification and compliance that would foster long-term strategic stability.

Structure of the Treaty and Associated Documents

The Treaty consisted of a **main text (17 Articles)** and **nine integral documents**, each legally binding and essential to the Treaty's enforceability.

Main Treaty Text (Articles I–XVII)

The core treaty lays out:

Definitions (Article I)

Limits on strategic arms (Article II)

Non-circumvention clauses (Article IV)

Compliance and verification mechanisms (Articles IX–XII)

Duration and withdrawal (Articles XV–XVI)

Associated Protocols and Annexes

Annex on Definitions and Categories Referenced in Article I: Defines essential terms such as "deployed ICBM," "throw-weight," "heavy bomber," etc.

Inspection Protocol (with 12 Annexes): Referenced in Article XI and Article XII: Outlines 12 types of inspections (e.g., baseline, elimination, suspect-site), personnel limits, procedures for access, and timelines. Clause: **Article XI, Paragraphs 11–12**, governs the requirement and structure of inspections prior to treaty entry into force.

Notification Protocol, Referenced in Article XIII: Requires detailed notifications for any movement, elimination, deployment, or modification of strategic offensive arms.

Throw-weight Protocol, Referenced in Article IV and the Definitions Annex Limits each side's throw-weight capacity (especially of ICBMs and SLBMs) and standardizes methods for its measurement.

Telemetry Protocol, Referenced in Article IX: Mandates open broadcast of telemetry during flight tests and **prohibits encryption** that would prevent full data sharing.

Conversion or Elimination Protocol, Referenced in Article VIII: Establishes verifiable physical procedures for converting or destroying strategic systems.

Joint Compliance and Inspection Commission (JCIC) Protocol, Referenced in Article XV: Establishes the JCIC to resolve compliance disputes and implement agreed changes to the treaty.

Memorandum of Understanding (MOU), Referenced in Article IV and Annexes Provides initial and updated declarations of forces, facility locations, technical data, missile attributes, etc.

Supplementary Agreements and Commitments

In addition to the core documents, four politically binding agreements and seven legally binding letters clarified implementation issues and extended treaty obligations.

Four Related Agreements (Referenced in JCIC records and legal annexes):

- Early exhibitions of strategic arms (based on **Article XI** and Inspection Protocol)

- Early inspector/aircrew list exchanges (tied to **Section II of Inspection Protocol**)

- Site diagrams and coordinates (support for the MOU)

- Advance notification of major strategic exercises (based on **Article XIII, Paragraph 2**)

Seven Letters Between Delegation Heads, these include:

- The phased reduction of heavy ICBMs

- Verification of Bear D bombers (TU-95RTs)

- Clarification of B-1 bomber classification While not part of the main treaty body, these letters are acknowledged under **Article XV (JCIC authority)** and were signed in parallel with the treaty, making them legally binding.

Central Limits – Article II

Article II of the Treaty establishes strict caps on strategic nuclear forces:

Article II, Paragraph 1: Limits deployed ICBMs, SLBMs, and heavy bombers to **1,600 delivery vehicles**.

Article II, Paragraph 2: Limits **warheads** attributed to those vehicles to **6,000 total**, with the following sublimits:

- No more than **4,900** on deployed ICBMs and SLBMs
- No more than **1,540** on heavy ICBMs

- No more than **1,100** on mobile ICBMs

Article II, Paragraph 4: Limits the **aggregate throw-weight** of ICBMs and SLBMs to levels **approximately 50% below** the Soviet baseline as of 1988.

Verification and Accountability Regime
START's verification provisions were among the most comprehensive ever negotiated:

On-Site Inspections: Article XI, Paragraphs 1–14
Includes:

- Baseline data inspections

- Reentry vehicle inspections

- Continuous monitoring of mobile ICBM production

- Elimination and conversion inspections

- Suspect site inspections

Data Exchanges: Article IV, Paragraphs 1–3: Regular sharing of:

- Force structure and technical data

- Deployment locations and launcher status

- Warhead loadings and delivery vehicle characteristics

National Technical Means (NTM):

- **Article IX:** Each side was allowed to use NTM (e.g., satellite reconnaissance) to monitor the other's compliance.
- **Article IX, Paragraph 1**: Prohibits concealment and interference with NTM. **Article IX, Paragraph 2**: Requires cooperative measures to enhance verification (e.g., distinguishability of systems).

Telemetry Access: Article IX, Paragraph 3 and Telemetry Protocol

Bans encryption or suppression of flight test data, enabling real-time verification of missile characteristics and warhead counts.

Continuous Monitoring:

Article XI, Paragraph 5 and Annex IV of the Inspection Protocol

Allows permanent presence of inspectors at specified mobile ICBM assembly and deployment facilities.

Treaty Duration and Withdrawal

- **Article XVI**: The Treaty was to remain in force for **15 years**, renewable in **5-year increments**.

- **Article XV, Paragraph 4**: Allows withdrawal with **6 months' notice** if "extraordinary events" jeopardize a party's national interests.

The START Treaty was not merely a bilateral disarmament agreement — it was a multilayered legal and verification architecture, designed to reduce nuclear risk, ensure predictability, and institutionalize transparency. Each article and protocol served a specific function in what became a historic model for future arms control, including New START (2010).

Effectiveness and Breaches

The Strategic Arms Reduction Treaty (START I), signed on July 31, 1991, and entering into force on December 5, 1994, was a landmark agreement between the United States and the Soviet Union (later Russia) aimed at reducing and limiting strategic offensive arms. Over its duration, the treaty achieved significant milestones in nuclear disarmament, though it also faced challenges and controversies.

Effectiveness of START I

Upon its enforcement, both the United States and Russia committed to substantial reductions in their strategic arsenals:

- United States: Reduced its deployed strategic warheads Attributed to Deployed ICBMs and

SLBMs and Deployed Heavy Bombers to approximately 5,949 by 2001 and 5,576 by January 2009 from 8,824 in December 1994, adhering to the treaty's stipulations limit of 6000[85]. Additionally, it reduced the deployed ICBMs and SLBMs and their associated launchers and deployed heavy bombers to 1,238 in December 2001 from 1,848 in December 1994 and to 1,198 by January 2009 to comply with the limit of 1,600 stipulated in the treaty[86].

- Russia: Lowered its deployed strategic warheads attributed to Deployed ICBMs and SLBMs and Deployed Heavy Bombers to about 5,518 in 2001 and 3,309 in January 2009 from 9,548 in December 1994, meeting its obligations under the treaty[87]. Additionally, it reduced the deployed ICBMs and SLBMs and their associated launchers and deployed heavy bombers to 1,136 in December 2001 from 1,958 in December 1994 and to 814 by January 2009 to comply with the limit of 1,600 stipulated in the treaty[88].

---

[85] The Legacy of START and Related U.S. Policies - https://2009-2017.state.gov/t/avc/rls/126119.htm
[86] The Legacy of START and Related U.S. Policies - https://2009-2017.state.gov/t/avc/rls/126119.htm
[87] The Legacy of START and Related U.S. Policies - https://2009-2017.state.gov/t/avc/rls/126119.htm
[88] The Legacy of START and Related U.S. Policies - https://2009-2017.state.gov/t/avc/rls/126119.htm

These reductions marked a significant step toward diminishing the nuclear threat and enhancing global security.

Inclusion of Former Soviet States:

A notable aspect of START I was its extension to former Soviet republics possessing nuclear weapons: Belarus, Kazakhstan, and Ukraine: These nations, upon gaining independence, inherited portions of the Soviet nuclear arsenal. Under the treaty's framework, they agreed to transfer all nuclear warheads to Russia and accede to the Nuclear Non-Proliferation Treaty (NPT) as non-nuclear-weapon states.

Verification Measures:

START I established rigorous verification protocols to ensure compliance:

- On-Site Inspections: Both parties conducted regular inspections of each other's facilities to monitor adherence.

- Data Exchanges: Comprehensive exchanges of information regarding the number, location, and technical characteristics of strategic systems were mandated.

- Telemetry Sharing: The treaty required the sharing of missile test telemetry to promote transparency.

These measures built mutual trust and set a precedent for future arms control agreements.

Breaches and Controversies

Despite its successes, START I encountered several challenges:

Mobile Intercontinental Ballistic Missiles (ICBMs):

A point of contention was the deployment and verification of mobile ICBMs:

- U.S. Position: Advocated for strict limitations and robust verification mechanisms for mobile ICBMs, citing concerns over their potential to destabilize strategic balance.

- Soviet/Russian Position: Argued that mobile ICBMs enhanced survivability and served as a credible second-strike capability.

This disagreement highlighted differing strategic doctrines and complicated negotiations.

Anti-Ballistic Missile (ABM) Treaty Withdrawal:

In 2002, the United States withdrew from the 1972 ABM Treaty, which had been a cornerstone of strategic stability:

Russian Reaction: Viewed the U.S. withdrawal as a threat to the strategic balance and expressed concerns over the potential development of missile defence systems undermining deterrence.

It is worth noting that the Soviet government made a unilateral statement in 1991, when the START treaty was signed. The Soviet government said it would be justified in withdrawing from the START Treaty if the United States withdrew from the Anti-Ballistic Missile Treaty (ABM Treaty). As it happened, in 2001 the United States did withdraw from the ABM Treaty. The Russian government objected, but did not withdraw from the START Treaty[89].

Intermediate-Range Nuclear Forces (INF) Treaty Violations:
Allegations of violations further strained arms control efforts:

- U.S. Allegations (2014): Accused Russia of violating the INF Treaty by developing and testing a ground-launched cruise missile (GLCM) with a prohibited range.

- Russian Response: Denied the allegations and, in turn, accused the U.S. of deploying systems in

---

[89] A New START in Prague | whitehouse.gov -
https://obamawhitehouse.archives.gov/blog/2010/04/07/a-new-start?utm_source

Europe that could be adapted for offensive purposes, potentially breaching the treaty.

Expiration and Succession:

START I officially expired on December 5, 2009. To continue the momentum of nuclear reductions, the United States and Russia negotiated the New Strategic Arms Reduction Treaty (New START), which was signed on April 8, 2010, and entered into force on February 5, 2011. This treaty built upon the foundations of START I, implementing further reductions and continuing verification measures.

In summary, while START I was a pivotal treaty that achieved significant reductions in nuclear arsenals and established comprehensive verification mechanisms, it also faced challenges related to differing strategic priorities, treaty compliance issues, and evolving geopolitical dynamics. The legacy of START I underscores the complexities inherent in arms control agreements and the continuous effort required to adapt to changing international security environments.

Legacy of the START Treaty

Though START I would not enter into force until December 5, 1994—delayed by the collapse of the Soviet Union and subsequent ratification hurdles in the newly independent republics—it still emerged as a cornerstone in global nuclear diplomacy. The Treaty was more than a legal mechanism for reducing arms. It was a symbolic and practical milestone, marking a shift from nuclear brinkmanship toward mutual restraint, verification, and transparency.

A Monument to Diplomacy

START I was born out of Cold War anxiety, but it was guided by a new strategic ethic: that the two most powerful nations on Earth could mutually reduce weapons, rather than increase them. By the time it was signed in 1991, the Cold War was ending, but the vast arsenals built over decades still posed a grave threat.

"It signalled a turning point in U.S.-Soviet arms control efforts toward a more rational, open, cooperative, predictable and stable relationship.[90]" George H.W. Bush and Mikhail Gorbachev Joint Statement, June 1, 1990

Delay and Determination

Despite the Treaty being signed in 1991, it took over three years to enter into force due to geopolitical upheaval:

---

[90] Soviet-United States Joint Statement on the Treaty on Strategic Offensive Arms | The American Presidency Project - https://www.presidency.ucsb.edu/documents/soviet-united-states-joint-statement-the-treaty-strategic-offensive-arms?utm_source

- The dissolution of the Soviet Union in December 1991 required renegotiation with Russia, Ukraine, Belarus, and Kazakhstan—all of which inherited portions of the Soviet nuclear arsenal.
- These states eventually joined the Nuclear Non-Proliferation Treaty (NPT) as non-nuclear-weapon states and transferred their warheads to Russia under the Lisbon Protocol to START I.

Establishing a Model of Arms Control

START I's true legacy is that it became the template for future arms control agreements, including:

- **New START (2010)**, which preserved and updated many of START I's verification protocols

- Confidence-building mechanisms that endure to this day, such as **Data exchanges** on missile and bomber deployments, **On-site inspections and Telemetry sharing**

START I remains the foundation on which all subsequent strategic arms control efforts have been built.

Institutional and Legal Innovations

START introduced or normalized several key features in international arms control:

Legal Frameworks for Reductions

START was the first treaty to require **actual reductions**, not just limits or freezes. It mandated:

- The **destruction or conversion** of delivery systems (per the Conversion/Elimination Protocol)

- Verification of destruction through **joint inspections and data confirmations**

The Joint Compliance and Inspection Commission (JCIC)

Established under **Article XV**, the JCIC provided an ongoing forum for:

- Clarifying treaty obligations

- Resolving compliance disputes

- Updating verification practices

Normalization of Nuclear Transparency

Prior to START, nuclear capabilities were shrouded in secrecy. The Treaty institutionalized:

- Baseline force data exchanges (Article IV)

- Recurrent updates

- National Technical Means (NTM) use with a ban on concealment (Article IX)

Strategic and Political Impact

Confidence Building

By embedding transparency into treaty practice, START served as a strategic trust mechanism. It was particularly significant during:

- Russia's turbulent post-Soviet transition in the 1990s

- Periods of U.S.-Russia diplomatic strain, where inspections continued regardless of political tension

Diplomatic Legacy

START helped codify a post-Cold War nuclear order where:

- Arms control became institutional rather than ideological

- Compliance could be verified by science and procedure rather than political goodwill

Perhaps most importantly, it gave humanity a glimpse of what cooperation could look like in a world divided not by ideology, but by mutual fear.

START I did not just reduce nuclear arms, it redefined the way the world approaches nuclear stability, showing that transparency, dialogue, and verification can succeed even after decades of rivalry.

START II: The Treaty That Almost Was — A Tale of Promise and Fallout

In the final chapters of the Cold War, a historic opportunity emerged. The world stood at the edge of a new era — no longer consumed by the tension of nuclear brinkmanship but instead daring to imagine disarmament. It was the early 1990s, and the iron grip of Soviet power had loosened. Out of the shadows of ideological warfare, two men — U.S. President George H. W. Bush and Russian President Boris Yeltsin — dared to dream big.

On a crisp January 3, 1993, in Moscow, these two leaders came together and signed what was heralded as a monumental step toward global security: the Strategic Arms Reduction Treaty II, (START II).

The U.S. Senate ratified the treaty in January 1996, but Russia Duma postponed for years until ratifying the treaty in April 2000.

In a conference with President Yeltsin in Moscow on April 21, 1996 and following five hours discussions with President Clinton, the U.S. president states:

"Russian and American missiles are no longer pointed at each other's cities or citizens. We've both made deep cuts in our nuclear arsenals by putting START I into force. And we'll make even deeper cuts when the Duma ratifies START II"[91].

---

[91] The President's News Conference With President Boris Yeltsin of Russia in Moscow | The American Presidency Project -

The Mission of START II

Unlike its predecessor, START I — which had already begun chipping away at the mountain of nuclear arms — START II aimed to strike at the core of the Cold War's deadliest legacy: *MIRVed ICBMs* (Multiple Independently Targetable Reentry Vehicles mounted on Intercontinental Ballistic Missiles)[92]. These weapons were not just symbols of power; they were instruments of terrifying first-strike potential.

By December 31, 2002, START II would have imposed the following mandates on each party including that:

- The total number of deployed strategic warheads could not exceed 3,500

- No warhead could be downloaded onto ICBMs or heavy ICBMs with MIRV capabilities

- No ICBM with MIRV capabilities could be deployed

---

https://www.presidency.ucsb.edu/documents/the-presidents-news-conference-with-president-boris-yeltsin-russia-moscow-1?utm_source
[92] Strategic Arms Reduction Treaty II - Center for Arms Control and Non-Proliferation - https://armscontrolcenter.org/strategic-arms-reduction-treaty-ii/

- No more than 1,750 warheads could be deployed on SLBMs, but there was no prohibition on SLBMs with MIRV capability[93]

START II vs. START I: What Changed?

Where START I (signed in 1991) focused on limits — capping strategic warheads at 6,000 — START II was revolutionary. It didn't just limit; it eliminated.

	START I (1991)	START II (1993)
Parties	U.S. & Soviet Union	U.S. & Russia
Focus	Reduce total warhead numbers and delivery vehicles	Enhance strategic stability by removing first-strike weapons
Warhead Limit	Max of 6,000 deployed strategic nuclear warheads	Reduced to 3,000–3,500 deployed warheads
Delivery Vehicles	1,600 total delivery systems (ICBMs, SLBMs, bombers)	Same ceiling of 1,600 delivery vehicles
MIRVed ICBMs	Allowed (with limits)	Banned — all MIRVed ICBMs to be eliminated
Heavy ICBMs (e.g., SS-18)	Permitted within the limit	Eliminated entirely
Verification Measures	Extensive on-site inspections, data exchanges, telemetry sharing	Built upon START I's verification system
Entry into Force	Entered into force December 5, 1994	Signed but never entered into force

---

[93] Strategic Arms Reduction Treaty II - Center for Arms Control and Non-Proliferation - https://armscontrolcenter.org/strategic-arms-reduction-treaty-ii/

The Collapse: A Dream Deferred

Despite its promise, START II was never destined to live long. The U.S. Senate ratified the treaty swiftly in January 1996, but Russia hesitated. The mood had shifted. NATO was expanding eastward — toward Russia's doorstep. And tensions were flaring over U.S. actions in Iraq and Kosovo.

The Russian Duma delayed for years, finally ratifying the treaty in April 2000, but with strings attached: implementation was conditioned on the preservation of the Anti-Ballistic Missile (ABM) Treaty. That treaty — from the Cold War era — limited missile defence systems to preserve the strategic balance.

Then came the breaking point: the administration of the United States of America under President George W. Bush announced on 13th December 2001 that it is withdrawing from the 1972 Anti-Ballistic Missile Treaty with six months' notice, seeking to build missile defences against rogue states.

Russia responded in kind — formally withdrawing from START II on June 14, 2002, effectively killing the agreement.

"However, we consider it a mistake... I can say that the decision made by the President of the United States does not threaten Russia's national security[94]," said Vladimir Putin (Russia President).

Legacy and Lessons

Though START II never entered into force, its negotiation was not in vain. It pushed the dialogue on first-strike stability, and its principles influenced later agreements — notably the New START Treaty, signed in 2010 and still (as of 2024) in effect.

It also left behind a sobering reminder: arms control is as much about trust and politics as it is about numbers and treaties.

Chapter Conclusion: The Beginning of the End of the End

In the chill of a Reykjavik autumn, two men sat across a table from one another—each commanding the most destructive arsenal in human history. Reagan's gaze was steely but hopeful. Gorbachev, earnest but wary. Between them lay decades of mutual suspicion, a Cold War's worth of animosity, and more than 60,000 nuclear weapons.

---

[94] Russian President Vladimir Putin's response to the U.S. decision to withdraw from the ABM treaty -
https://www.atomicarchive.com/resources/documents/missile-defense/putin-abm-remarks.html?utm_source

They didn't leave Iceland with a treaty. They left with something rarer: the outline of a world where treaties could matter again.

From those tense hours in 1986 came a seed—fragile yet determined—that would take root through years of negotiation, military skepticism, political infighting, and the collapse of an empire. When the START Treaty was finally signed in the vaulted grandeur of the Kremlin in 1991, it carried with it the ambitions of statesmen, the caution of generals, and the hope of billions.

And yet, the ink was barely dry when the Soviet Union— one of its signatories—ceased to exist.

But START endured.

It adapted. It was ratified. It was implemented. And over the next decade, missile silos were sealed. Bombers were retired. Warheads were removed. Two superpowers, forged in confrontation, began the process of dismantling the very engines of Armageddon—not with war, but with words.

By 2001, thousands of strategic warheads had been verifiably eliminated. The U.S. had reduced its deployed warheads to 5,948, and Russia to 5,518, meeting the treaty's hard limits. On-site inspections unfolded in former enemy territory. U.S. inspectors stood on Russian soil; Russian monitors watched American weapons being taken apart. Trust was no longer a gamble. It was protocol.

More than any technical detail or clause, START's legacy is this: it made transparency possible. It made trust procedural. And in a time when ideological divides had driven humanity to the brink of annihilation, it showed that even the most bitter rivals could sit, reason, verify, and act—for the common good.

It wasn't perfect. Disputes over missile defense and mobile ICBMs exposed how fragile consensus could be. The U.S. withdrawal from the ABM Treaty in 2002 sent tremors through the arms control regime. But START had already done its work. It created the vocabulary, the inspection culture, the bilateral commissions, and the verification standards that would be inherited by its successor, New START, in 2010.

START was not the end of nuclear danger. But it was the beginning of the end of the age when numbers grew unchecked and missiles remained faceless monsters in secret bunkers.

In a world still haunted by the possibility of nuclear conflict, the START Treaty remains a benchmark of what is possible when diplomacy is persistent, when verification is rigorous, and when the will to survive becomes stronger than the will to dominate.

In that, START wasn't merely a treaty between two states. It was a treaty with history itself.

Chapter (8)

A New START: A Treaty Forged in Hope and History

"While the New START treaty is an important first step forward, it is just one step on a longer journey"

Barak Obama (U.S. President)

As the world entered the second decade of the 21st century, two former Cold War superpowers—the United States and the Russian Federation—stood at a crossroads. Years of strained relations, mutual suspicion, and strategic one-upmanship had left their mark. The original START I Treaty, signed in 1991, had expired in 2009, and though it had ushered in historic nuclear reductions, the absence of a successor left a dangerous vacuum.

With global nuclear tensions simmering and emerging threats on the horizon, both nations saw the need to rekindle cooperation. Under the leadership of President Barack Obama and President Dmitry Medvedev, negotiations gave birth to a new hope: The New START Treaty, signed on April 8, 2010, in Prague.

"Today is an important milestone for nuclear security and non-proliferation, and for U.S.-Russia relations[95]." **President Barack Obama**, Signing Ceremony, April 2010.

Ceremony of signing the NEW START

On April 8, 2010, a pivotal moment in international diplomacy unfolded within the historic halls of Prague Castle in the Czech Republic, where U.S. president Barak Obama and the Russian president Dmitry Medvedev convened to sign the New Strategic Arm Reduction Treat (New Start).

Setting the Scene: Prague Castle

Prague Castle, an emblem of Czech heritage, provided a grand backdrop for the ceremony. Its centuries-old architecture bore witness to this contemporary stride toward global security. The choice of Prague was symbolic; just a year prior, President Obama had articulated his vision for a world free of nuclear weapons in this very city[96]. He emphasized on April 5, 2009:

---

[95] Remarks by President Obama and President Medvedev of Russia at New START Treaty Signing Ceremony and Press Conference | whitehouse.gov -
https://obamawhitehouse.archives.gov/the-press-office/remarks-president-obama-and-president-medvedev-russia-new-start-treaty-signing-cere
[96] A New START in Prague | whitehouse.gov -
https://obamawhitehouse.archives.gov/blog/2010/04/07/a-new-start?utm

"I state clearly and with conviction America's commitment to seek the peace and security of a world without nuclear weapons. I'm not naive. This goal will not be reached quickly — perhaps not in my lifetime. It will take patience and persistence. But now we, too, must ignore the voices who tell us that the world cannot change. We have to insist, "Yes, we can.[97]"

"Now, let me describe to you the trajectory we need to be on. First, the United States will take concrete steps towards a world without nuclear weapons. To put an end to Cold War thinking, we will reduce the role of nuclear weapons in our national security strategy, and urge others to do the same. Make no mistake: As long as these weapons exist, the United States will maintain a safe, secure and effective arsenal to deter any adversary, and guarantee that defense to our allies — including the Czech Republic. But we will begin the work of reducing our arsenal.

To reduce our warheads and stockpiles, we will negotiate a new Strategic Arms Reduction Treaty with the Russians this year. President Medvedev and I began this process in London, and will seek a new agreement by the end of this year that is legally binding and sufficiently bold. And this will set the stage for further cuts, and we will seek to include all nuclear weapons states in this endeavour[98].

The Ceremony Unfolds

Dignitaries, diplomats, and international media gathered in anticipation. The atmosphere was charged with optimism as both leaders took their seats to formalize the

---

[97] The President in Prague | The White House -
https://obamawhitehouse.archives.gov/video/The-President-in-Prague/#transcript
[98] The President in Prague | The White House -
https://obamawhitehouse.archives.gov/video/The-President-in-Prague/#transcript

treaty. The act of signing was more than procedural; it represented a mutual commitment to a safer world.

Statements of Significance

Following the signing, both presidents addressed the assembly. President Obama emphasized:

"…, this day demonstrates the determination of the United States and Russia -- the two nations that hold over 90 percent of the world's nuclear weapons -- to pursue responsible global leadership. Together, we are keeping our commitments under the Nuclear Non-Proliferation Treaty, which must be the foundation for global non-proliferation.

While the New START treaty is an important first step forward, it is just one step on a longer journey. As I said last year in Prague, this treaty will set the stage for further cuts. And going forward, we hope to pursue discussions with Russia on reducing both our strategic and tactical weapons, including non-deployed weapons[99]".

President Medvedev in his turn shared the same views stating:

"A truly historic event took place: A new Russia-U.S. treaty has been signed for the further reduction and limitation of strategic offensive arms"…."As a result, we obtained a document that in full measure maintains the balance of interest of Russia and the United

---

[99] Remarks by President Obama and President Medvedev of Russia at New START Treaty Signing Ceremony and Press Conference | whitehouse.gov - https://obamawhitehouse.archives.gov/the-press-office/remarks-president-obama-and-president-medvedev-russia-new-start-treaty-signing-cere

States of America. What matters most is that this is a win-win situation. No one stands to lose from this agreement"…."This agreement enhances strategic stability and, at the same time, enables us to rise to a higher level for cooperation between Russia and the United States[100]"

Global Implications

The New START Treaty mandated significant reductions in deployed strategic nuclear warheads and delivery systems for both nations. Its signing was hailed globally as a step forward in nuclear disarmament and non-proliferation efforts. The ceremony in Prague not only marked the culmination of extensive negotiations but also set the tone for future collaborative security endeavors.

In essence, the signing ceremony of the New START Treaty at Prague Castle was a historic event that underscored the importance of diplomacy and mutual commitment in addressing global security challenges.

The Treaty's Purpose: Predictability, Parity, Peace

The New START Treaty — formally titled the *"Treaty between the United States of America and the Russian Federation*

---

[100] Remarks by President Obama and President Medvedev of Russia at New START Treaty Signing Ceremony and Press Conference | whitehouse.gov -
https://obamawhitehouse.archives.gov/the-press-office/remarks-president-obama-and-president-medvedev-russia-new-start-treaty-signing-cere

on Measures for the Further Reduction and Limitation of Strategic Offensive Arms" — had a bold vision: to reduce deployed nuclear weapons while preserving strategic stability and enhancing transparency. The United States and the Russian Federation have agreed to extend the treaty through February 4, 2026.

Its goals were simple yet profound:

- Limit the number of deployed strategic nuclear warheads.

- Cap the delivery systems that could launch them.

- Build mutual trust through regular inspections and data sharing.

It wasn't just about numbers—it was about resetting trust between two nuclear giants.

What the Treaty Limits

Strategic Offensive Limits: The New START Treaty entered into force on February 5, 2011. Under the treaty, the United States and the Russian Federation had seven years to meet the treaty's central limits on strategic offensive arms (by February 5, 2018) and are then obligated to maintain those limits for as long as the treaty remains in force[101].

---

[101] New START Treaty - United States Department of State - https://www.state.gov/new-start-treaty

Aggregate Limits: Both the United States and the Russian Federation met the central limits of the New START Treaty by February 5, 2018, and have stayed at or below them ever since. Those limits are:

- 700 deployed intercontinental ballistic missiles (ICBMs), deployed submarine-launched ballistic missiles (SLBMs), and deployed heavy bombers equipped for nuclear armaments.

- 1,550 nuclear warheads on deployed ICBMs, deployed SLBMs, and deployed heavy bombers equipped for nuclear armaments (each such heavy bomber is counted as one warhead toward this limit);

- 800 deployed and non-deployed ICBM launchers, SLBM launchers, and heavy bombers equipped for nuclear armaments[102].

How New START Differs from START I (1991)

I summarized in the following table what I believed some of the key differences between START (1991) treaty and the new START (2010) treaty to give a flavour of the progress made over years between both nuclear power houses.

---

[102] New START Treaty - United States Department of State - https://www.state.gov/new-start-treaty

Feature	START I (1991)	New START (2010)
Warhead Limit	6,000 deployed strategic nuclear warheads	1,550 deployed strategic nuclear warheads
Delivery Vehicles Limit	1,600 (ICBMs, SLBMs, heavy bombers)	700 deployed (plus 800 total, including non-deployed)
Treaty Duration	15 years (with extension option)	10 years, extended in 2021 to 2026
Verification Regime	Highly detailed and intrusive: 12 types of inspections and massive data exchanges	Streamlined: up to 18 inspections per year, data updates, unique identifiers (UIDs)
Missile Defense Link	No mention or limits on missile defense	Acknowledges offense-defense relationship, but imposes no limits
Parties Involved	United States and USSR (later Russia, Ukraine, Belarus, Kazakhstan)	United States and Russian Federation
On-site inspection	Up to 70 per year	Up to 18 per year
Data Exchanges	Extensive (over 2,000 pages of site-specific data in first exchange)	Simplified, periodic database with updates and notifications
Scope of Reductions	Reduced stockpiles but retained large arsenals	Aimed for deeper reductions and more modern transparency tools
Multilateral Impact	Only bilateral, focused on Cold War arms race	Envisioned as a step toward broader non-proliferation, NPT-compliant

Effectiveness of the NEW START in reducing both nuclear power houses threats

Since its entry into force on February 5, 2011, the New START Treaty has been instrumental in promoting transparency and predictability between the world's two largest nuclear powers. The treaty's key achievements include:

- **Reduction of Deployed Strategic Nuclear Warheads:** Both nations have reduced their deployed strategic nuclear warheads to the treaty's limit of 1,550.

- **Limitation of Delivery Vehicles:** The treaty restricts each side to 700 deployed intercontinental ballistic missiles (ICBMs), submarine-launched ballistic missiles (SLBMs), and heavy bombers, with an additional limit of 800 deployed and non-deployed launchers and bombers.

- **Verification Measures:** The treaty established a robust verification regime, including on-site inspections and data exchanges, fostering trust and compliance.

The U.S. Department of State has consistently affirmed that the New START Treaty enhances U.S. national security by providing limits on Russian nuclear forces and offering transparency and predictability[103].

Latest Aggregate Data from New START

As of the latest publicly available data, the United States and Russia have reported their strategic offensive arms within the treaty's limits[104]. However, it's important to

---

[103] 2022 - Report On The Reasons That Continued Implementation Of The New START Treaty is in The National Security Interest Of The United States - United States Department of State - https://www.state.gov/report-on-the-reasons-that-continued-implementation-of-the-new-start-treaty-is-in-the-national-security-interest-of-the-united-states/?utm
[104] 2023 Report to Congress on Implementation of the New START Treaty - United States Department of State - https://www.state.gov/bureau-of-arms-control-deterrence-and-

note that on February 21, 2023, Russia announced it was suspending its participation in the New START Treaty. Despite this, the United States has continued to release its aggregate data voluntarily[105].StateState+1State+1

According to the U.S. Department of State's fact sheet dated May 12, 2023, the United States reported the following[106]:

- Deployed ICBMs, SLBMs, and Heavy Bombers: 662

- Warheads on Deployed ICBMs, Deployed SLBMs, and Nuclear Warheads Counted for Deployed Heavy Bombers: 1,419

- Deployed and Non-Deployed Launchers of ICBMs, SLBMs, and Deployed and Non-Deployed Heavy Bombers: 800

These figures demonstrate the United States' commitment to adhering to the treaty's limits, even amidst geopolitical challenges.

The New START Treaty has been effective in curbing the nuclear capabilities of both the United States and Russia, thereby contributing to global strategic stability.

---

stability/releases/2024/01/2023-report-to-congress-on-implementation-of-the-new-start-treaty

[105] New START Treaty Aggregate Numbers of Strategic Offensive Arms - United States Department of State - https://www.state.gov/new-start-treaty-aggregate-numbers-of-strategic-offensive-arms-5/?utm_

[106] New START Treaty Aggregate Numbers of Strategic Offensive Arms - United States Department of State - https://www.state.gov/new-start-treaty-aggregate-numbers-of-strategic-offensive-arms-5/?utm

The latest data reflects compliance with the treaty's provisions, underscoring its role as a cornerstone of international arms control efforts.

Tensions & Challenges Amidst the Optimism of the New START

The initial optimism surrounding the New START Treaty in 2010 gradually diminished due to escalating geopolitical tensions and strategic disagreements between the United States and Russia. Here's an in-depth examination of the key events that contributed to this shift:

2014: Ukraine Crisis and Crimea Annexation

In the post-Cold War era, NATO expanded eastward, incorporating several former Eastern Bloc countries. This expansion was perceived by Russia as a direct threat to its sphere of influence and national security. The prospect of Ukraine joining NATO was particularly alarming to Moscow, given Ukraine's strategic importance and shared border with Russia.

Euromaidan Protests and Political Upheaval

In late 2013, Ukrainian President Viktor Yanukovych's decision to reject an association agreement with the European Union in favor of closer ties with Russia sparked massive protests, known as the Euromaidan movement. These demonstrations culminated in February 2014 with Yanukovych's ousting. The political upheaval created a power vacuum and heightened tensions between pro-European and pro-Russian factions within Ukraine.

Annexation of Crimea

In the aftermath of Ukraine's political turmoil, unmarked Russian troops seized control of key infrastructure in Crimea in late February 2014. Despite initial denials, Russia later acknowledged these forces as its own. A controversial referendum was held in March 2014, resulting in a declaration of independence from Ukraine and subsequent annexation by Russia. This move was widely condemned internationally and led to the imposition of sanctions against Russia

Eastern Ukraine Conflict

Following the annexation of Crimea, pro-Russian separatists in eastern Ukraine's Donbas region declared independence, leading to armed conflict with Ukrainian forces. Russia's support for these separatists further strained relations with the West and deepened the crisis.

International Response

The annexation of Crimea and the conflict in eastern Ukraine prompted widespread international condemnation and led to economic sanctions against Russia. NATO increased its presence in Eastern Europe, citing the need to reassure member states and deter further Russian aggression.

In summary, the Ukraine crisis and Crimea's annexation were driven by a combination of NATO's eastward expansion, Russia's strategic interests, internal Ukrainian political dynamics, and historical ties between Russia and Ukraine.

Disagreements Over Missile Defense, Hypersonic Weapons, and Space Militarization

During this period, several strategic disagreements further strained relations:

Missile Defense: The U.S. continued to develop and deploy missile defence systems, which Russia perceived as a threat to its nuclear deterrent[107].

Hypersonic Weapons: Both nations pursued the development of hypersonic weapons, leading to concerns about a new arms race.

The Trump administration's 2019 Missile Defense Review argued the need for an improved capability to intercept cruise and hypersonic missiles, including long-range strikes targeting the continental United States. The Biden administration's 2022 Missile Defense Review acknowledged these concerns. The Missile Defense Agency is managing several new programs to improve hypersonic missile defense, such as the Hypersonic and Ballistic Tracking Space Sensor and the Glide-Phase

---

[107] Current U.S. Missile Defense Programs at a Glance | Arms Control Association - https://www.armscontrol.org/factsheets/current-us-missile-defense-programs-glance

Interceptor. U.S. Northern Command and the MDA have done limited tests and studies on improving homeland defence against cruise missiles.

The 2022 Missile Defense Review restated the traditional U.S. policy that Ground Mid-Course Defense (GMD) is *"neither intended nor capable of defeating the missile capabilities of Russia and China"*. The review also reaffirmed *"the interrelationship between strategic offensive arms and strategic defensive systems"*. It also emphasized, for the first time, the lower-tier threat posed by unmanned aircraft systems[108].

Space Militarization: The establishment of the U.S. Space Force and discussions about deploying weapons in space raised alarms about the potential weaponization of space. The U.S. Space Force (USSF) was established on Dec. 20, 2019, creating the first new branch of the armed services since 1947. The establishment of the USSF resulted from widespread recognition that space is a national security imperative[109].

These issues complicated efforts to negotiate extensions or replacements for existing arms control treaties, including New START.

---

[108] Current U.S. Missile Defense Programs at a Glance | Arms Control Association -
https://www.armscontrol.org/factsheets/current-us-missile-defense-programs-glance
[109] https://www.spaceforce.mil/About-Us/

2023: Russia's Suspension of New START Participation

Amidst the ongoing conflict in Ukraine, Russian President Vladimir Putin announced on February 21, 2023, that Russia would suspend its participation in the New START Treaty. He stated:

"They want to inflict a 'strategic defeat' on us and try to get to our nuclear facilities at the same time[110]".

Putin argued that while the U.S. has pushed for the resumption of inspections of Russian nuclear facilities under the treaty, NATO allies had helped Ukraine mount drone attacks on Russian air bases hosting nuclear-capable strategic bombers[111].

"The drones used for it were equipped and modernized with NATO's expert assistance,"…. "And now they want to inspect our defense facilities? In the conditions of today's confrontation, it sounds like sheer nonsense"… "In this regard, I am compelled to announce today that Russia is suspending its membership in the New START Treaty[112]".

---

[110] en.kremlin.ru - https://en.kremlin.ru/events/president/news/70565

[111] Putin says Russia suspending participation in New START treaty, last nuclear weapons pact with U.S. - CBS News - https://www.cbsnews.com/news/russia-putin-us-nuclear-weapons-treaty-new-start-suspending-articipation/#:~:text=Moscow%20%E2%80%94%20Russian%20President%20Vladimir%20Putin%20declared%20Tuesday,tensions%20with%20Washington%20over%20the%20fighting%20in%20Ukraine.

[112] en.kremlin.ru - https://en.kremlin.ru/events/president/news/70565

This move further undermined the last remaining arms control agreement between the two largest nuclear powers.

The announcement from Putin drew criticism from Secretary of State Antony Blinken, who called it *"deeply unfortunate and irresponsible"*… "We'll be watching carefully to see what Russia actually does," … "We'll of course make sure that in any event, we are postured appropriately for the security of our own country and that of our allies.[113]"

The United States expressed concern over Russia's decision but chose not to withdraw from the treaty, aiming to preserve the framework for strategic arms control. The U.S. Department of State emphasized the importance of the treaty for global security and expressed hope for Russia's return to compliance.

Legacy: Fragile But Foundational

The **New START Treaty** stands as a pivotal pillar in the architecture of global nuclear arms control, symbolizing a rare beacon of cooperation between the United States and Russia amidst a landscape often marred by rivalry. Despite enduring numerous challenges, it remains the last major arms control agreement binding the two largest nuclear powers.

---

[113] Putin says Russia suspending participation in New START treaty, last nuclear weapons pact with U.S. - CBS News

A Fragile Legacy

The treaty's significance is underscored by its role in maintaining strategic stability. However, its fragility is evident as it approaches expiration in February 2026, with no successor agreement in sight. The potential lapse of New START could usher in an era of unchecked nuclear competition, reminiscent of the Cold War's perilous arms race. The Arms Control Association warns that without a replacement, there would be no constraints on the number of nuclear warheads the U.S. and Russia can deploy, heightening global security risks[114].

Official Endorsements

The treaty has garnered explicit support from U.S. leadership. In 2021, Secretary of State Antony Blinken emphasized its critical role, stating:

"Extending the New START Treaty ensures we have verifiable limits on Russian ICBMs, SLBMs, and heavy bombers until February 5, 2026.[115]"

A Testament to Cooperation

Beyond its technical provisions, New START embodies the possibility of collaboration between historical adversaries. In a world increasingly defined by polarization, the treaty serves as a testament to reason and

---

[114] Recommendations for Congressional Priorities on Nuclear Weapons & Arms Control Policy During the 119th Congress | Arms Control Association -
https://www.armscontrol.org/Recommendations-for-Congressional-Priorities-2025?utm
[115] New START at a Glance | Arms Control Association -
https://www.armscontrol.org/factsheets/new-start-glance?utm

mutual interest. Its existence proves that even amidst profound differences, dialogue and agreement on matters of existential importance are achievable.

Looking Ahead

As the expiration date looms, the international community faces a critical juncture. The potential dissolution of New START without a successor could destabilize global nuclear order. The Arms Control Association highlights that failure to reach a new agreement may lead to an unconstrained arms race, with both nations capable of rapidly expanding their arsenals.

In conclusion, while the New START Treaty's legacy is fragile, it remains foundational to global arms control. Its preservation and extension are imperative to prevent a regression into a more perilous era of nuclear competition

Chapter Conclusion: Echoes of Trust in a World of Tension

In the candlelit halls of Prague Castle, as signatures dried on parchment and history quietly shifted beneath pen strokes, a rare moment of global optimism took shape. The New START Treaty was more than a document—it was a declaration that even the bitterest rivals could forge a common vision for peace.

Forged by leaders who dared to imagine a future unshackled from Cold War fears, the treaty represented **a**

bold recommitment to strategic sanity. President Barack Obama called it "an important milestone for nuclear security," and Russian President Dmitry Medvedev hailed it as "a win-win" for both nations. The world listened, and for a moment, it believed.

But as history has taught us, hope must often wrestle with hard reality.

In the years that followed, the seeds of renewed distrust were quietly sown. The **2014 annexation of Crimea**, NATO's evolving presence in Eastern Europe, and the **race for hypersonic dominance** all reshaped the strategic calculus. The **formation of the U.S. Space Force**, along with new defense doctrines, further deepened Russia's unease. Dialogue slowed. Shadows lengthened.

By **February 21, 2023**, President Vladimir Putin stood before his nation and uttered the words that marked a breaking point:

"I am compelled to announce today that Russia is suspending its membership in the New START Treaty."

His reasoning is that the U.S. and NATO sought to "inflict a strategic defeat" on Russia and could not be trusted with access to sensitive nuclear sites during wartime.

The United States, though shaken, **did not withdraw**. Secretary of State **Antony Blinken** called the move "deeply unfortunate and irresponsible," but affirmed America's commitment to the treaty's ideals:

"Extending the New START Treaty ensures we have verifiable limits on Russian ICBMs, SLBMs, and heavy bombers until February 5, 2026."

In that statement, and in the U.S.'s continued data transparency—even after Russia's suspension—lay the final ember of the treaty's spirit: trust, however tenuous.

Today, **New START remains the last thread of legal restraint** tethering the world's two largest nuclear powers to a framework of accountability. It is battered, bruised, and bloodied by geopolitics—but it is not yet broken.

If the world allows this agreement to unravel, it risks stepping back into a world where **nuclear arsenals grow unchecked**, where warheads outpace diplomacy, and where fear—not foresight—drives security.

But if the spirit of Prague endures—if the echo of that moment in 2010 can find new life—then perhaps a new chapter can still be written. A chapter not of rivalry, but of reason. Not of escalation, but of restraint.

For in the arc of global history, **treaties are more than ink on paper**. They are promises across divides. Promises we cannot afford to forget.

Chapter (9)

Eyes in the Sky — The Treaty on Open Skies and the Tug of Titans

"Open Skies will strengthen international stability... and provide an important means of increasing mutual understanding."

President George H. W. Bush

The Geopolitical Scene: A World in Transition

The early 1990s were a turning point in the 20th century — the Cold War had ended, the Iron Curtain had been lifted, and a new world order was being forged in the embers of old rivalries. Across Europe, former Soviet satellite states tasted the first winds of independence, and the mighty USSR had just crumbled, leaving the Russian Federation in its place — dazed, yet determined to redefine its role.

In this fragile landscape, trust was as rare as peace had been during the Cold War. Mistrust still hung heavy in the air. Could the world's most powerful military forces find a new way to coexist?

Enter the **Treaty on Open Skies** — an idea that had been buried in Cold War archives for decades but, finally, found fertile ground.

The concept was first proposed by **President Dwight D. Eisenhower** in Geneva in July of 1955 at the Four Power (U.S., USSR, UK, and France) Summit, a bold vision of transparency: allow each other's planes to fly over military installations to reduce the chance of war by miscalculation. The Soviets balked at the time. But history, as it often does, circled back.

By **1989**, with Soviet reforms under Mikhail Gorbachev and the West advocating for openness, U.S. President George H. W. Bush revived the idea — this time, as a multilateral proposal, not just bilateral.

Formal talks began in Ottawa in 1990, continued in Budapest, and finally culminated in Vienna in 1991, after the failed August coup in Moscow softened Russian resistance. At long last, the Treaty on Open Skies was signed on March 24, 1992, in Helsinki.

"Open Skies will strengthen international stability… and provide an important means of increasing mutual understanding." President George H. W. Bush, Letter to the U.S. Senate, August 1992[116].

---

[116] Open Skies Treaty - https://2009-2017.state.gov/t/avc/trty/102337.htm

Purpose and the Nations That Joined Hands

The treaty had a singular goal: to build trust through transparency.

By permitting unarmed aerial surveillance over each other's entire territories, participating countries could observe military forces and installations directly — not through hearsay or satellites, but by soaring above, cameras rolling.

The Treaty on Open Skies was signed on March 24, 1992, by 27 countries, encompassing both NATO and former Warsaw Pact members. The original signatories included nations such as the United States, Russia, Ukraine, Belarus, Canada, France, Germany, and the United Kingdom. Over time, the treaty expanded to include 34 countries in total. However, following the withdrawals of the United States in 2020 and Russia in 2021, 32 countries currently remain parties to the treat[117]

You probably can't imagine the fact that the United States can fly an unarmed military reconnaissance airplane anywhere over Russia and thirty-two other treaty signatory nations with only twenty-four hours' notice of the intended flight plan. Equally, the Russian Federation has the right to conduct aerial photography flights over the United States and other treaty members[118].

---

[117] Treaty on Open Skies - Federal Foreign Office - https://www.auswaertiges-amt.de/en/aussenpolitik/themen/218432-218432?utm
[118] Open Skies: Transparency, Confidence-Building, and the End of the Cold War on JSTOR - https://www.jstor.org/stable/j.ctvqsdq9x

The area it covered? From Vancouver to Vladivostok, making it one of the broadest arms-control efforts in modern history.

"The Treaty on Open Skies represents the widest-ranging international effort to date to promote openness and transparency." **James A. Baker III**, U.S. Secretary of State. [119]

The Machinery of Transparency: Key Elements of the Treaty

The Treaty on Open Skies was more than a diplomatic handshake — it was a technical, meticulously structured framework that gave form to the abstract idea of trust. Below, we dive into the critical features of the treaty, guided by its clauses and annexes, to understand how the world's most sophisticated surveillance accord actually worked.

Territorial Transparency (Article VI & Article I)

Perhaps the boldest feature of the treaty was its promise of complete territorial openness. According to **Article I, Section 1**, the treaty established a regime of aerial observation flights over the entire territory of each participating state. No areas could be made off-limits for national security reasons — a historical departure from Soviet-era secrecy.

---

[119] Open Skies Treaty - https://2009-2017.state.gov/t/avc/trty/102337.htm

Only one exception was allowed: air safety. As clarified in Article VI, Section I (14–15), flights were subject to International Civil Aviation Organization (ICAO) standards and local air traffic control instructions. National sovereignty was respected, but secrecy was no longer a shield.

"Whereas the former Soviet Union had insisted on closing areas... the Treaty provides that only flight safety considerations may restrict observation flights." U.S. State Department[120].

Observation Aircraft and Sensor Limitations (Articles IV & V)

The treaty permitted only unarmed, fixed-wing aircraft, as per Article V, Section 1. These aircraft, either provided by the observing or observed party, were required to undergo rigorous certification to verify sensor specifications.

Clause **Article IV, Section 1** lists four types of permissible sensors:

- Optical panoramic and framing cameras

- Video cameras with real-time display

- Infra-red line-scanning devices

- Side-looking synthetic aperture radar (SAR)

---

[120] Open Skies Treaty - https://2009-2017.state.gov/t/avc/trty/102337.htm

Sensor capabilities were strictly limited to prevent high-resolution spying. For example:

- **Optical cameras**: Max ground resolution of 30 cm (Article IV.2.a)

- **Infrared scanners**: Max resolution of 50 cm (Article IV.2.c)

- **SAR**: Resolution limited to 3 meters using impulse response (Article IV.2.d)

All equipment had to be commercially available to ensure transparency and equal access (Article IV.1).

Sensor upgrades or new technologies could be proposed and negotiated through the Open Skies Consultative Commission (OSCC) under **Article X**.

"Photographic image quality will permit recognition of major military equipment... allowing significant transparency of military forces." - U.S. Treaty Letter of Transmittal[121]

Quota System for Flights (Article III & Annex A)

Observation rights were balanced through a **quota system**. Each country agreed to a passive quota (number of flights it must accept) and an active quota (number it may conduct), detailed in **Article III**.

---

[121] Open Skies Treaty - https://2009-2017.state.gov/t/avc/trty/102337.htm

- The **United States and Russia/Belarus**: 42 annual flights each (Annex A, Section I)

- Smaller countries like Iceland or Luxembourg: 2–4 annual flights

- Clause **Article III.5** ensures that a nation can't conduct more flights than it agrees to receive.

Additionally, countries could transfer or share quotas with other parties under **Article III.9**, encouraging collaboration and flexibility.

"Each State Party shall have the right to conduct... a number of observation flights equal to those conducted over it." Treaty, Article III.3[122].

Flight Planning and Mission Execution (Article VI)

Observation flights followed carefully structured procedures:

- Notification: Observing party must give **72 hours' notice** before arrival (Article VI.5)

- Flight Duration: Missions must be completed within **96 hours** of arrival (Article VI.9)

- Mission Plan: Submitted on arrival and approved within **4 hours** (Article VI, Section II.6)

---

[122] Open Skies Treaty - https://2009-2017.state.gov/t/avc/trty/102337.htm

- Flights must follow the **approved flight plan**, and any deviation must be justified by weather, emergencies, or safety (Article VIII.2)

The observed party had the right to provide their own aircraft and crew (**Article VI.1**), but the observing state could also bring its own certified aircraft.

"Observation flights shall take priority over regular air traffic." - Article VI.14[123]

Data Sharing and Transparency (Article IX)

The treaty established rules for handling and sharing surveillance data. Under **Article IX**:

- Film and digital data must be sealed immediately after flight (Section I.3)

- Observed and observing parties both receive copies

- Other parties can request copies (Section IV)

To prevent tampering or espionage, no transmission of data was allowed during the flight (Article IX.2). All sensor output had to be stored onboard and reviewed post-mission.

---

[123] Open Skies Treaty - https://2009-2017.state.gov/t/avc/trty/102337.htm

Film development protocols, duplication quality, and annotation procedures are detailed in **Annex K** and **Annex B**.

"Data collected... shall be made available to other States Parties upon request."- Article IX, Section IV[124].

Dispute Resolution: The OSCC (Article X)

The **Open Skies Consultative Commission (OSCC)**, established under **Article X**, serves as the treaty's governing and oversight body. Based in Vienna, the OSCC is tasked with:

- Reviewing implementation and compliance

- Addressing complaints and technical issues

- Admitting new members by consensus

The OSCC operates on unanimous consensus, ensuring that every state party has a voice — and a veto. "The OSCC shall take decisions... by consensus." - Article X.2[125].

---

[124] Open Skies Treaty - https://2009-2017.state.gov/t/avc/trty/102337.htm
[125] Open Skies Treaty - https://2009-2017.state.gov/t/avc/trty/102337.htm

Was It Effective? Trust, Tension, and Turbulence

In the years following its ratification, the Treaty on Open Skies fulfilled its promise of enhancing transparency and trust among its member states. From its entry into force in 2002 up until October 2019, over **1,500 observation flights** were conducted[126], allowing nations to monitor military activities and verify compliance with arms control agreements.

These missions were not merely symbolic; they provided real-time, firsthand visual data on troop movements, military exercises, and potential buildups. This capability was particularly beneficial for smaller countries, granting them access to strategic intelligence that would have been challenging to obtain independently[127].

However, by the late 2010s, tensions began to surface. The United States accused Russia of violating the treaty by imposing restrictions on observation flights over certain regions. Specifically, Russia limited flight distances over the **Kaliningrad Oblast** to 500 kilometres and denied flights within 10 kilometres of portions of the Georgian Russian border. In the Department of Defense statement May 21, 2020, the DOD statement explained:

---

[126] The Open Skies Treaty: Background and Issues | Congress.gov | Library of Congress - https://www.congress.gov/crs-product/IN10502
[127] The Open Skies Treaty at a Glance | Arms Control Association - https://www.armscontrol.org/factsheets/openskies?utm

"Russia has also continuously violated its obligations under the Treaty, despite a host of U.S. and Allied efforts over the past several years. Since 2017, the United States has declared Russia in violation of the Treaty for limiting flight distances over the Kaliningrad Oblast to 500 kilometers (km) and for denying flights within 10 km of portions of the Georgian-Russian border. Most recently, in September 2019, Russia violated the Treaty again by denying a flight over a major military exercise, preventing the exact transparency the Treaty is meant to provide[128].

In response to these alleged violations, the U.S. announced its intention to formally submit its notification to withdraw from the treaty on 22 May 2020, with the withdrawal becoming effective on November 22, 2020[129].

Following the U.S. departure, Russia expressed concerns about the imbalance created by the withdrawal and initiated its own process to exit the treaty. Russia's withdrawal was formalized on June 7, 2021, when President Vladimir Putin signed the law completing the process[130].

[128] DOD Statement on Open Skies Treaty Withdrawal > U.S. Department of Defense > Release - https://www.defense.gov/News/Releases/Release/Article/2195239/dod-statement-on-open-skies-treaty-withdrawal/
[129] DOD Statement on Open Skies Treaty Withdrawal > U.S. Department of Defense > Release - https://www.defense.gov/News/Releases/Release/Article/2195239/dod-statement-on-open-skies-treaty-withdrawal/
[130] Putin signs law taking Russia out of Open Skies arms control treaty | Reuters - Putin signs law taking Russia out of Open Skies arms control treaty | Reuters

The Kremlin that the U.S. decision to withdraw from the treaty had "*significantly upset the balance of interests*" among the pact's members and had compelled Russia to exit.

"*This caused serious damage to the treaty's observance and its significance in building confidence and transparency, (causing) a threat to Russia's national security,*"[131].

Despite the exit of these two major powers, the treaty remains in effect with **32 other member states** continuing their participation, upholding the principles of mutual observation and transparency.

Legacy of the Treaty: Eyes in the Sky, Lessons on the Ground

The **Treaty on Open Skies** stands not just as a clause-bound agreement, but as a *philosophical milestone* in arms control history. It was among the most innovative post-Cold War initiatives, not because it introduced cutting-edge technology or sweeping disarmament, but because it institutionalized something rare: mutual military transparency in real time, in shared space, with human presence.

At its core, the treaty embraced the radical idea that watching one another openly could build more peace than secrecy ever had. For the first time, adversaries flew over each other's territory — not as spies or invaders, but as

---

[131] https://en.kremlin.ru/events/president/news/65870?utm

invited observers, cameras in hand, collecting data to be shared. It proved that old adversaries could open their skies, and their secrets, to one another, and survive.

The **power of that image** — a Russian Tu-154 aircraft flying over the United States, or an American OC-135B over Russia — spoke louder than policy papers. It said: *We have nothing to hide.* That symbolism, wrapped in legal frameworks and safeguarded by technical clauses, showed what confidence-building can look like when backed by political will.

Even after the U.S. withdrawal in 2020 and Russia's in 2021, the treaty did not vanish into obsolescence. Over 30 nations remain parties to it, including key European powers like Germany, France, and the United Kingdom, who continue to view Open Skies as a vital confidence-building measure — particularly amid modern geopolitical frictions.

"The Treaty on Open Skies is an important element of the European security architecture. Germany, together with its partners, is committed to preserving the Treaty and continuing its full implementation" German Foreign Office 2020 Annual Disarmament Report[132].

---

[132] Jahresabrüstungsbericht 2020 - https://www.auswaertiges-amt.de/resource/blob/2457644/7a4fbb16352c3d2c3587fbc014ce6d4a/abrbericht2020-data.pdf

The Treaty's Subtle Power in a Shifting World

The irony is striking: at a time when drone warfare, satellite espionage, and AI-driven surveillance dominate headlines, the Treaty on Open Skies relied on something refreshingly human — pilots, observers, interpreters, and trust. Its value wasn't in spying better; it was in spying together, in the open, with both sides watching the watchers.

In a world trending toward strategic ambiguity, where nations deny cyber intrusions and mask troop movements behind misinformation, Open Skies stood as a stubborn counterexample. It said: *Clarity is still possible. Verification still matters. And sometimes, the most profound trust-building comes from simply being there — physically, visually, and jointly.*

The treaty also served as a model for regional transparency, one that arms control experts have suggested could be adapted for use in South Asia, the Middle East, or even the Korean Peninsula, where mutual suspicion continues to fester. Open Skies principles remain relevant beyond Europe. They could offer a trust-building model for regions where suspicion goes deep.

A Treaty Etched in the Sky — and in History

The treaty leaves behind the blueprint for openness in an age of concealment. It leaves the memory of enemy aircraft welcomed into domestic airspace, and the hope that such openness might someday return. Most of all, it leaves the lesson that arms control isn't just about counting missiles — it's about cultivating mutual confidence in a world that too often defaults to distrust.

In the end, the poetry of Open Skies wasn't just in its name — it was in its practice. For a moment in history, the sky was truly shared. And that may have been its greatest achievement of all.

Chapter Conclusion: Through the Clouds, Toward Clarity

History often finds its metaphors in the skies. For centuries, the air above us was a domain of myth, a place for gods and dreams. But in the modern era, it became something else entirely — a stage for power, a frontier of surveillance, and sometimes, a space for peace.

The **Treaty on Open Skies** was a bold attempt to reclaim that space for trust.

Born in the ashes of the Cold War, when suspicion was as dense as smog and the world's two superpowers had only just stepped back from the nuclear brink, the treaty offered a radical alternative: **to look, openly, without hostility — and to allow others to look back.**

It was, in many ways, the **first arms control agreement you could literally see** — observers flying together, logging images, watching the watchers. No spy satellites. No secret code. Just wings, windows, and rules.

For a generation, it worked. Over 1,500 flights. Thousands of images. Dozens of nations building a rhythm of cooperation. Even small states, normally shut out of high-level military affairs, could peer across borders and gain clarity — not from leaks, but from law.

And then came the unravelling.

Geopolitical shifts, accusations, strategic distrust — they began to cloud the skies again. When the U.S. exited in 2020, followed by Russia in 2021, it wasn't just a legal withdrawal. It was a retreat from a philosophy that had taken flight: that **transparency could be sovereign**, and that **security didn't have to mean secrecy**.

Yet, despite the thunder of exits, the treaty didn't crash.

Thirty-two nations still remain committed, still believe in the simple strength of showing, rather than hiding. Their flights may be fewer, and their impact diminished without the giants, but their message endures: *openness is not dead — it's just grounded, waiting for the right wind.*

In a world of faceless drones and shadow wars, where distrust often travels faster than diplomacy, the Treaty on Open Skies offered something profoundly human: **the courage to be visible**. It told us that **peace doesn't come from the absence of observation — it comes from its presence, mutual and honest.**

So as we close this chapter, we look not just at what was lost, but what was proven possible.

The skies may no longer be as open as they once were. But the idea remains — that perhaps the path to peace lies not in building higher walls, but in flying over them, together.

Chapter (10)

SORT – The Treaty that Whispered the End of an Era

"Russia is not an enemy; Russia is a friend"

George W. Bush (US President)

Prelude to a New Strategic Reality

The final decade of the 20th century marked a significant shift in the global order. The Cold War, which had long defined the geopolitical landscape through a rigid framework of nuclear deterrence and ideological rivalry, had ended with the collapse of the Soviet Union in 1991. In its place emerged a reconfigured world—still complex and dangerous, but less defined by the binary logic of mutually assured destruction. The United States and the Russian Federation remained the world's largest nuclear powers, yet their relationship was beginning to evolve.

By the turn of the millennium, both nations recognized the obsolescence of Cold War-era nuclear postures. The quantity and structure of their arsenals, designed for an existential standoff, no longer reflected the emerging security environment of the 21st century. New challenges—such as transnational terrorism, the proliferation of weapons of mass destruction, and regional instability—rose to the forefront. The events of **September 11, 2001**, in particular, underscored the necessity for broader cooperation and re-evaluation of strategic priorities.

It was against this backdrop that U.S. President **George W. Bush** and Russian President **Vladimir V. Putin** began a series of engagements that would catalyze a shift in arms control dialogue. The **first key breakthrough** came on **July 22, 2001**, during the **G8 Summit in Genoa, Italy**, where both leaders issued a **Joint Statement on Strategic Issues**:

"We agreed that major changes in the world require concrete discussions of both offensive and defensive systems. We already have some strong and tangible points of agreement. We will shortly begin intensive consultations on the interrelated subjects of offensive and defensive systems[133]".

This statement signalled a new willingness by both sides to engage in joint strategic recalibration, including

---

[133] The Moscow Treaty - https://2009-2017.state.gov/t/avc/trty/127129.htm#4

discussions on nuclear arms reductions and missile defence.

The momentum continued to build in the months that followed. At a **landmark summit on November 13, 2001**, in Washington, D.C., Presidents Bush and Putin issued a **Joint Statement on a New Relationship Between the United States and Russia**, affirming that:

"Our countries are embarked on a new relationship for the 21st century, founded on a commitment to the values of democracy, the free market, and the rule of law. The United States and Russia have overcome the legacy of the Cold War. Neither country regards the other as an enemy or threat[134]".

At the same press conference, President Bush acknowledged that existing U.S. nuclear force levels no longer aligned with strategic needs:

"The current levels of our nuclear forces do not reflect today's strategic realities. I have informed President Putin that the United States will reduce our operationally deployed strategic nuclear warheads to a level between 1,700 and 2,200 over the next decade, a level fully consistent with American security[135]".

---

[134] November 13, 2001 - Joint Statement by President George W. Bush and President Vladimir V. Putin on a New Relationship Between the United States and Russia - https://2009-2017.state.gov/t/avc/trty/127129.htm#4

[135] November 13, 2001 - Press Conference by President Bush and Russian President Vladimir Putin The East Room - https://2009-2017.state.gov/t/avc/trty/127129.htm#4

President Putin, addressing an audience at the **Russian Embassy in Washington** that same day, echoed the sentiment:

"Russia is stating its readiness to proceed with significant reductions of strategic offensive arms… at the least, by a factor of three—to the minimum level necessary to maintain strategic equilibrium in the world[136]".

In a further response on **December 13, 2001**, following the U.S. announcement of its withdrawal from the 1972 ABM Treaty, Putin emphasized the importance of codifying reductions:

"A particularly important task in these conditions is to legally formalize the agreements that have been reached on further drastic, irreversible, and verifiable reductions in strategic offensive arms, which we believe should be at the level of 1,500–2,200 nuclear warheads for each side[137]".

These exchanges between Bush and Putin—held over a span of just six months—culminated in the conception of what would become one of the **swiftest arms control treaties negotiated between the two nations**. The treaty, later known as the **Moscow Treaty on Strategic Offensive Reductions (SORT)**, would be signed in May 2002, less than a year after the Genoa summit. It signalled a decisive move away from Cold War mechanics and

---

[136] President Putin, for his part, stated at the Russian Embassy in Washington, DC on November 13, 2001 - https://2009-2017.state.gov/t/avc/trty/127129.htm#4
[137] President Putin, for his part, stated at the Russian Embassy in Washington on December 13, 2001 - https://2009-2017.state.gov/t/avc/trty/127129.htm#4

toward a leaner, more flexible approach to nuclear force management.

Signing in Moscow: Words That Moved the World

On **May 24, 2002**, in the gilded halls of the Kremlin, President **George W. Bush** and President **Vladimir V. Putin** signed the **Treaty on Strategic Offensive Reductions** (SORT), also known as the **Moscow Treaty**. Their signatures sealed not just a legal pact, but a symbolic end to an arms race that had once held the world hostage.

In his transmittal letter to the U.S. Senate, Bush wrote:

"The Moscow Treaty represents an important element of the new strategic relationship between the United States and Russia... Each country will be at the lowest level of deployed strategic nuclear warheads in decades[138]."

Putin echoed this hope, saying the treaty signaled that:

"we no longer need to frighten each other in order to arrive at agreements. Security is established... by the political will of states and of the leaders of these states.

Yes, today the world is still far from having international relations built exclusively upon trust. Unfortunately. That is why it is so

---

[138] LETTER OF TRANSMITTAL by George W. Bush – Addressed to the White House - June 20, 2002 – to the Senate of the United States - https://2009-2017.state.gov/t/avc/trty/127129.htm#4

important today to rely upon the existing foundation of treaties and agreements in the field of disarmament and arms control[139]."

Anatomy of the Treaty: Flexibility Meets Finality

At just five articles long, the **Moscow Treaty** was remarkably concise—but it carried heavy weight.

The purpose of the treaty was to reduce and limit the number of strategic nuclear warheads to between 1,700 and 2,200 for each side by December 31, 2012. The key elements of the treaty are as follows:

Flexibility of Force Structure (Article I)

At the heart of the treaty is **Article I**, which obligates both parties to reduce and limit their aggregate number of **strategic nuclear warheads to between 1,700 and 2,200** by **December 31, 2012**. However, unlike earlier agreements, SORT does not prescribe **how** these reductions should be achieved.

"Each Party shall determine for itself the composition and structure of its strategic offensive arms, based on the established aggregate limit for the number of such warheads[140]."

---

[139] Speech of Russian Federation President V. V. Putin to Representatives of the American Public and U.S. Politicians, November 13, 2001, Russian Embassy in Washington – Department of State Archive
[140] SORT – Article (1) - The Moscow Treaty - https://2009-2017.state.gov/t/avc/trty/127129.htm

This clause granted the United States and Russia **complete discretion** over the mix of intercontinental ballistic missiles (ICBMs), submarine-launched ballistic missiles (SLBMs), and strategic bombers that make up their respective nuclear triads. It also meant that downloaded warheads—removed from missiles but retained in storage—were not explicitly banned or required to be destroyed.

This approach stood in contrast to the **START I Treaty (1991)**, which employed detailed counting rules and mandated the elimination of delivery systems under strict verification protocols. By comparison, SORT's minimalism was both praised for its pragmatic adaptability and criticized for its potential reversibility.

No Independent Verification Regime (Article II)

While SORT imposed limits on warheads, it did not establish a standalone verification mechanism. Instead, Article II simply stated:

"The Parties agree that the START Treaty remains in force in accordance with its terms[141]."

Thus, SORT relied entirely on the 1991 START Treaty's verification regime, which included measures such as:

- On-site inspections

---

[141] SORT – Article II - The Moscow Treaty - https://2009-2017.state.gov/t/avc/trty/127129.htm

- Data exchanges

- Notification protocols

- Continuous monitoring

At the time of SORT's signing, START I was still active and effective. However, this reliance posed challenges as START I was set to expire in December 2009, and with it, SORT's only framework for mutual transparency and compliance assurance. Once START expired and until New START replaced it in 2011, there existed a verification gap, raising concerns among analysts and arms control advocates about the enforceability of SORT's commitments.

Oversight via the Bilateral Implementation Commission (Article III)

To facilitate dialogue and resolve potential disputes, **Article III** created a consultative mechanism:

"For purposes of implementing this Treaty, the Parties shall hold meetings at least twice a year of a Bilateral Implementation Commission[142]."

This Bilateral Implementation Commission (BIC) was conceived as a diplomatic forum, not a technical enforcement body. It lacked legal power to impose sanctions or amend the treaty. Its primary function was to

---

[142] SORT – Article III - The Moscow Treaty - https://2009-2017.state.gov/t/avc/trty/127129.htm

monitor progress, build confidence, and foster transparency through regular engagement.

This mechanism was modelled loosely on similar bodies from previous arms control agreements, but its limited mandate mirrored SORT's minimalist philosophy: emphasis on political goodwill over bureaucratic oversight.

Treaty Duration and Withdrawal Clause (Article IV)

SORT was designed with a **finite timeline**, but included a clause that granted each party significant latitude in withdrawing:

"This Treaty shall remain in force until December 31, 2012... Each Party, in exercising its national sovereignty, may withdraw from this Treaty upon three months written notice to the other Party[143]."

Unlike many arms control agreements that condition withdrawal on the emergence of **"extraordinary events" threatening national interests** - as seen in the **1972 ABM Treaty**, Article XV - SORT imposed **no such threshold**. This made the treaty **easily revocable**, reflecting the political rather than legalistic nature of the agreement.

---

[143] SORT, Article IV, Sections 2–3 - The Moscow Treaty - https://2009-2017.state.gov/t/avc/trty/127129.htm

A Record Low Limit — Without Destruction Requirements

While SORT established the lowest numerical ceiling for deployed strategic nuclear warheads ever agreed between the United States and Russia—between 1,700 and 2,200 warheads—it did not require the physical dismantlement of warheads or delivery systems.

This omission led to significant criticism from arms control observers. Unlike START I, which mandated the elimination of platforms (such as ICBM silos or bombers), SORT permitted the removal of warheads from launchers while allowing them to be retained in storage, potentially available for re-deployment.

As President Bush emphasized at the time, this reflected a new philosophy:

"There is no longer the need to narrowly regulate every step we each take, as did Cold War treaties founded on mutual suspicion and an adversarial relationship.[144]*"*

This design was intended to reflect the post–Cold War strategic environment, but it also meant that SORT lacked the irreversibility that characterized more robust treaties like START I or later New START (2010).

---

[144] LETTER OF TRANSMITTAL – George W. Bush - June 20, 2002 - To the Senate of the United States - The Moscow Treaty - https://2009-2017.state.gov/t/avc/trty/127129.htm#4

In summary, the Strategic Offensive Reductions Treaty marked a watershed moment in U.S.–Russia arms control—legally simple, politically symbolic, and unprecedented in its flexibility. It created a framework for reductions, not a blueprint for disarmament. Its success depended not on detailed regulation, but on the continued political alignment and mutual trust between the two nuclear superpowers. While it achieved its numerical goals, SORT left unresolved the deeper issues of verification, irreversibility, and long-term stability—issues that would return to the forefront in the treaties that followed.

Reality Check: Effectiveness and Erosion

By 2012, both countries had met the target range. The U.S., guided by the Pentagon's **Nuclear Posture Review**, deactivated its **Peacekeeper ICBMs**, reduced its **Trident submarines**, and restructured its nuclear triad. Russia likewise met the limits, largely through aging out or decommissioning old Soviet-era systems.

Reduction Progress and Compliance

From the treaty's entry into force on **June 1, 2003**, until its termination on **February 5, 2011**, SORT mandated that both the U.S. and Russia reduce their operationally deployed strategic nuclear warheads to between 1,700 and 2,200 by December 31, 2012 as seen in article I of the treaty.

U.S. Reduction Milestones:

2005: The number of U.S. operationally deployed strategic nuclear warheads was 3878 as of December 31, 2005. The classified version of this Report contains the numbers of U.S. operationally deployed strategic nuclear warheads, by category of system, and estimated numbers of Russian Federation strategic nuclear warheads as of December 31, 2005[145]

2006: As of December 31, 2006, the United States reduced the number of operationally deployed strategic nuclear warheads to 3696. The classified version of this Report describes planned U.S. strategic offensive reductions in greater detail; it also describes the U.S. estimate of planned Russian strategic offensive reductions during 2006, based on information provided by Russia[146]

2007: The number of U.S. operationally deployed strategic nuclear warheads was 2871 as of December 31, 2007. The classified version of this Report contains the numbers of U.S. operationally deployed strategic nuclear warheads, by category of system, and estimated numbers of Russian Federation strategic nuclear warheads as of December 31, 2007[147].

2008: The number of U.S. operationally deployed strategic nuclear warheads was 2,246 as of December 31, 2008. The

---

[145] 2006 Annual Report on Implementation of the Moscow Treaty - https://2009-2017.state.gov/t/avc/rls/rpt/108870.htm
[146] 2007 Annual Report on Implementation of the Moscow Treaty - https://2009-2017.state.gov/t/avc/rls/rpt/88187.htm
[147] 2008 Annual Report on Implementation of the Moscow Treaty - https://2009-2017.state.gov/t/avc/rls/rpt/104637.htm

classified version of this Report contains the numbers of U.S. operationally deployed strategic nuclear warheads, by category of system, and estimated numbers of Russian Federation strategic nuclear warheads as of December 31, 2008[148].

2009: The number of U.S. operationally deployed strategic nuclear warheads was 1,968 as of December 31, 2009. The classified version of this Report contains the numbers of U.S. operationally deployed strategic nuclear warheads (ODSNW) by category of system, and estimated numbers of Russian Federation strategic nuclear warheads as of December 31, 2009[149]

2010–2011: The aggregate number of United States operationally deployed strategic nuclear warheads (ODSNW) was 1,941 as of December 31, 2010. The aggregate number of U.S. ODSNW was 1,944 as of February 5, 2011, the final day that the Moscow Treaty was in force. The classified version of this Report contains the numbers of U.S. ODSNW by category of system, and estimated numbers of Russian Federation strategic nuclear warheads as of December 31, 2010, and February 5, 2011[150].

---

[148] 2009 Annual Report on Implementation of the Moscow Treaty - https://2009-2017.state.gov/t/avc/rls/rpt/127122.htm
[149] 2010 Annual Report on Implementation of the Moscow Treaty - https://2009-2017.state.gov/t/avc/rls/rpt/141429.htm
[150] 2011 Annual Report on Implementation of the Moscow Treaty - https://2009-2017.state.gov/t/avc/rls/rpt/164828.htm

The U.S. strategic force structure for 2012 was planned to include[151]:

- 14 Trident SSBNs

- 450 Minuteman III ICBMs

- 20 B-2 Bombers

- 76 B-52H Bombers.

Russian Compliance Estimates

The implementation reports issued on the execution of the treaty consistently stated that the U.S. lacked full visibility into Russia's specific reduction plans or accounting method, as Russia did not disclose force structure details publicly. Nevertheless, the U.S. classified estimates and insights from START inspections supported the assessment that Russia was on track to meet its obligations.

The treaty implementation reports emphasized that Russia had the right to use a different counting method, and that SORT reductions were not required to mirror START counting rules.

---

[151] 2010 Annual Report on Implementation of the Moscow Treaty - https://2009-2017.state.gov/t/avc/rls/rpt/141429.htm

Verification and Oversight

SORT did not contain its own verification mechanism (unlike START). Instead, Article II maintained reliance on the existing START Treaty mechanisms. However, START expired in December 2009, creating a verification gap during SORT's final two years as explained before.

Despite the lack of specific verification provisions in SORT:

- The U.S. Administration relied on national intelligence capabilities and the transparency achieved under START to monitor Russian compliance.

- There was no formal mechanism to compel data exchange or validate reductions beyond START's expiration.

Article III of SORT established the **Bilateral Implementation Commission (BIC)**. It functioned as a diplomatic forum where the U.S. and Russia:

- Met at least twice per year (e.g., meetings in Geneva, 2006–2009)

- Exchanged briefings on force structures and plans

Effectiveness and Limitations

- **Numerical Reductions Achieved:** The U.S. met the treaty's upper limit of 2,200 warheads by 2010—two years ahead of schedule.

- **Lower Cap Achieved:** The 1,700–2,200 ceiling was the lowest ever agreed between the two powers up to that time.

However limitations clearly existed, some of these are:

- **No Warhead Destruction Required:** The treaty allowed warheads to be removed from deployment but kept in storage, potentially available for rapid redeployment.

- **Verification Deficit (Post-2009):** After START expired, there were no legally binding verification measures.

- **Ambiguity in Russian Data:** The U.S. repeatedly noted the **lack of transparency** in Russian force declarations and methodology.

- **No Enforcement Mechanism:** SORT had no penalties or accountability process for non-compliance or failure to meet reduction goals.

Despite its weaknesses, no breaches or violations were officially recorded in the reports. The United States continued to express confidence that Russia was likely meeting its reduction obligations, based on:

- Dialogue through the BIC

- Information from START (until 2009)

- Intelligence assessments

Final Phase and Succession

SORT was officially superseded by the New START Treaty on February 5, 2011[152]. The 2011 Implementation Report confirms that both sides were in compliance and had made substantial reductions by that time:

- U.S. deployed warheads: **1,944** on Feb 5, 2011[153]

- The treaty's goals were effectively met, but its legacy was shaped as much by its limitations as its achievements.

Legacy: A Candle in the Nuclear Wind

The **Strategic Offensive Reductions Treaty (SORT)**, or **Moscow Treaty**, occupies a unique and often understated place in the chronology of nuclear arms control. Though short in text and limited in technical mandates, its legacy was not measured in pages or

---

[152] 2011 Annual Report on Implementation of the Moscow Treaty - https://2009-2017.state.gov/t/avc/rls/rpt/164828.htm
[153] 2011 Annual Report on Implementation of the Moscow Treaty - https://2009-2017.state.gov/t/avc/rls/rpt/164828.htm

protocols — but in the rare geopolitical space it helped preserve.

A Bridge Across a Tumultuous Decade

Signed less than a year after the September 11, 2001 terrorist attacks, SORT emerged in a global atmosphere of heightened uncertainty. As the United States redirected its focus toward non-state threats and asymmetric warfare, traditional strategic dialogues could have easily been sidelined.

Yet, the Moscow Treaty ensured that U.S.–Russia nuclear relations remained on the diplomatic agenda. It served as a stabilizing force at a time when both nations were reassessing their global roles, military doctrines, and alliance systems. It allowed both sides to continue reductions in offensive arms without the burden of a Cold War-era verification bureaucracy, keeping momentum alive while new strategies were developed.

In this way, SORT was not just a policy tool — it was a political placeholder that kept nuclear dialogue intact during a decade of shifting priorities.

A Precursor to a More Robust Future

Although it lacked binding enforcement mechanisms or destruction requirements, SORT laid critical groundwork for the New START Treaty, signed in Prague on April 8, 2010, and entered into force in 2011.

Where SORT provided political consensus, New START provided technical substance:

- It reinstated on-site inspections, data exchanges, and conversion limits on delivery vehicles.

- It introduced a new warhead limit (1,550 deployed), building upon SORT's 1,700–2,200 range.

- It offered the structure and verification mechanisms that arms control experts had found lacking in SORT.

Without SORT, New START might have lacked the strategic trust and continuity needed for its negotiation and ratification. In this sense, the Moscow Treaty was a diplomatic scaffolding—lightweight, yet vital for constructing the architecture that followed.

From Adversaries to Strategic Stakeholders

Perhaps most symbolically, the Moscow Treaty was the first bilateral nuclear agreement in which both Russia and the United States publicly stated that they no longer viewed each other as enemies.

In the **2001 joint statement** that led to the treaty, both nations declared they had *"overcome the legacy of the Cold War"* and shared *"a new relationship for the 21st century."* That rhetorical pivot was **enshrined in the very character of SORT** — a document that required no intrusive checks, because it was built not on suspicion, but on mutual assurances.

This subtle but significant departure from past treaties redefined the tone of strategic arms negotiations, if not the technical rigor. It marked a transition from "containment" to cooperative reduction, even if such cooperation was politically rather than legally reinforced.

A Testament to Personal Diplomacy

In the annals of arms control, the Moscow Treaty is often remembered for what it did not do — but equally, it should be remembered for how it was done.

Where **START II** languished in legislative deadlock, bogged down by ratification hurdles and verification minutiae, SORT was negotiated, signed, and implemented with extraordinary speed. Within less than a year, Presidents George W. Bush and Vladimir Putin transitioned from dialogue to ratified treaty.

There were no detailed annexes, no complex sub-treaties — just a five-article commitment sealed by political will and strategic necessity. In this way, SORT represented a rare triumph of personal diplomacy over institutional inertia.

It reminded the international community that breakthroughs in arms control can come not only from

Global Hegemony: A Strategic Illusion

the intricacies of legal language, but from direct dialogue between leaders willing to recalibrate their worldviews.

In Retrospect

Though later overshadowed by more ambitious treaties, SORT's legacy remains critical:

- It prevented a vacuum in arms control during a volatile era.

- It reduced deployed nuclear warheads to historic lows.

- It demonstrated that strategic stability does not always require legal maximalism but can sometimes be nurtured through minimalism grounded in trust.

In a world still shadowed by nuclear risk, the Moscow Treaty stands as a quiet but enduring signal — that even in the aftermath of global trauma, reduction is possible, dialogue is valuable, and restraint is achievable.

Conclusion: The Soft Power of Strategic Restraint

The Moscow Treaty did not roar its presence with sweeping disarmament mandates or intrusive enforcement regimes. Instead, it arrived with the quiet confidence of mutual intent—an agreement born not of urgency, but of opportunity. It emerged at a rare inflection point when two former Cold War rivals found reason to turn from confrontation toward cooperation, and it gave shape to that fragile moment with the language of restraint.

In its sparseness, SORT invited criticism. It was modest in scope, it relied on old frameworks for verification, and it allowed the temporary storage—rather than elimination—of warheads. But what it lacked in technical precision, it made up for in strategic symbolism and diplomatic utility. In the wake of 9/11, in a world facing asymmetric and unpredictable threats, SORT ensured that nuclear arms control remained active—relevant, flexible, and forward-looking.

Its greatest accomplishment may well be the space it preserved: a diplomatic bridge that carried the United States and the Russian Federation through a transitional decade and into the era of New START. In that sense, SORT was never designed to be the destination. It was the corridor—the necessary pause between legacy and renewal, allowing trust to be tested and political will to be proven.

In the history of nuclear arms agreements, some treaties echo with the gravity of their pages. SORT whispers—but its voice is one of intent, pragmatism, and possibility. And sometimes, it is in the whisper—not the shout—that the world hears the first true sign of change.

References

1. Rare Chance to View Original NATO Treaty | National Archives - https://www.archives.gov/press/press-releases/2019/nr19-42?

2. 20161130_19490404__Opening_address_Truman-s.pdf - https://www.nato.int/nato_static_fl2014/assets/pdf/history_pdf/2016 1130_19490404__Opening_address_Truman-s.pdf?

3. Address on the Occasion of the Signing of the North Atlantic Treaty | The American Presidency Project - https://www.presidency.ucsb.edu/documents/address-the-occasion-the-signing-the-north-atlantic-treaty?

4. Malta summit ends the cold war – archive, 1989 | Europe | The Guardian - Https://www.theguardian.com/world/2024/nov/27/malta-summit-ends-the-cold-war-archive-1989?

5. Excerpts of Address by Mikhail Gorbachev. 43rd U.N. General Assembly Session, December 7, 1988 - Excerpts of Address by Mikhail Gorbachev. 43rd U.N. General Assembly Session, December 7, 1988

6. U.S. Department of State, FOIA 199504567 (National Security Archive Flashpoints Collection, Box 38) - https://nsarchive.gwu.edu/briefing-book/russia-programs/2017-12-12/nato-expansion-what-gorbachev-heard-western-leaders-early

7. Memorandum of conversation between Mikhail Gorbachev and Helmut Kohl - Mikhail Gorbachev i germanskii vopros, edited by Alexander Galkin and Anatoly Chernyaev, (Moscow: Ves Mir, 2006) - https://nsarchive.gwu.edu/briefing-book/russia-programs/2017-12-12/nato-expansion-what-gorbachev-heard-western-leaders-early

8. U.S. Embassy Bonn Confidential Cable to Secretary of State on the speech of the German Foreign Minister: Genscher Outlines His Vision of a New European Architecture.- U.S. Department of State. FOIA Reading Room. Case F-2015 10829

9. Mr. Hurd to Sir C. Mallaby (Bonn). Telegraphic N. 85: Secretary of State's Call on Herr Genscher: German Unification.- Documents on British Policy Overseas, series III, volume VII: German Unification, 1989-1990. (Foreign and Commonwealth Office. Documents on British Policy Overseas, edited by Patrick Salmon, Keith Hamilton, and Stephen Twigge, Oxford and New York, Routledge 2010). pp. 261-264 -

10. Ambassador Rodric Braithwaite diary, 05 March 1991- https://nsarchive.gwu.edu/briefing-book/russia-programs/2017-12-12/nato-expansion-what-gorbachev-heard-western-leaders-early

11. Record of conversation between Mikhail Gorbachev and Francois Mitterrand (excerpts) - Mikhail Gorbachev i germanskii vopros, edited by Alexander Galkin and Anatoly Chernyaev, (Moscow: Ves Mir, 2006), pp. 454-466

12. Letter from Mr. Powell (N. 10) to Mr. Wall: Thatcher-Gorbachev memorandum of conversation - Documents on British Policy Overseas, series III, volume VII: German Unification, 1989-1990. (Foreign and Commonwealth Office. Documents on British Policy Overseas, edited by Patrick Salmon, Keith Hamilton, and Stephen Twigge, Oxford and New York, Routledge 2010), pp 411-417

13. Letter from Mr. Powell (N. 10) to Mr. Wall: Thatcher-Gorbachev memorandum of conversation - Documents on British Policy Overseas, series III, volume VII: German Unification, 1989-1990. (Foreign and Commonwealth Office. Documents on British Policy Overseas, edited by Patrick Salmon, Keith Hamilton, and Stephen Twigge, Oxford and New York, Routledge 2010), pp 411-417

14. Valentin Falin Memorandum to Mikhail Gorbachev (Excerpts) - Mikhail Gorbachev i germanskii vopros, edited by Alexander Galkin and Anatoly Chernyaev, (Moscow: Ves Mir, 2006), pp. 398-408

15. Memorandum to Boris Yeltsin from Russian Supreme Soviet delegation to NATO HQs - State Archive of the Russian Federation (GARF), Fond 10026, Opis 1

16. NATO Speech by Pres. Clinton - 22 Oct. 1996 - https://www.nato.int/docu/speech/1996/s961022a.htm#:~:text=But%20mark%20my%20words%2C%20if,later%20on%20down%20the%20road.

17. Retranslation of Yeltsin letter on NATO expansion | National Security Archive - https://nsarchive.gwu.edu/document/16376-document-04-retranslation-yeltsin-letter

18. Yeltsin Letter to Clinton | National Security Archive - https://nsarchive.gwu.edu/document/27163-doc-09-yeltsin-letter-clinton

19. NATO Press Release NAC-S(99)64 - 24 April 1999 - https://www.nato.int/docu/pr/1999/p99-064e.htm?

20. NATO - Opinion: Remarks by US President George W. Bush at the NATO Accession Ceremony in Washington D.C., USA, 29-Mar.-2004 - https://www.nato.int/cps/en/natohq/opinions_21295.htm?selectedLocale=en

21. Stay away, Vladimir Putin tells Nato – https://www.telegraph.co.uk/news/worldnews/1584027/Stay-away-Vladimir-Putin-tells-Nato.html?msockid=105a39b5d5fb67fd2ca52c9bd440663a&ICID=continue_without_subscribing_reg_first

22. Russia threatens retaliation as Montenegro becomes 29th NATO member | Reuters - https://www.reuters.com/article/us-usa-nato-montenegro-idUSKBN18W2WS/

23. North Macedonia Joins the NATO Alliance - United States Department of State - https://2017-2021.state.gov/north-macedonia-joins-the-nato-alliance/?

24. NATO - News: Sweden officially joins NATO , 07-Mar.-2024 - https://www.nato.int/cps/en/natohq/news_223446.htm?

25. Russian news agency - NATO's 'reckless' expansion to undermine chances for security dialogue — Lavrov - Russian Politics & Diplomacy - TASS - https://tass.com/politics/1618823?fbclid=IwAR3E48ZS4zmHFHrUE RipqQ-sb9xa2r9sIbmvp4Fc7UGhXV8unrR1FCc-Psk%2Famp&utm_source

26. https://www.iaea.org/about/overview/history

27. https://www.iaea.org/about/overview/history

28. https://issforum.org/articlereviews/66-iaea

29. https://www.iaea.org/about/governance/list-of-member-states

30. IAEA statue

31. https://www.wsj.com/world/russia/nuclear-war-risks-rise-again-stoked-by-global-conflicts-fa3333b6

32. https://www.wsj.com/world/russia/nuclear-war-risks-rise-again-stoked-by-global-conflicts-fa3333b6

33. https://www.reuters.com/world/europe/un-nuclear-chief-visit-russian-atomic-plant-near-front-line-2024-08-27/

34. reuters.com/world/europe/key-facts-chornobyl-nuclear-plant-2025-02-14

35. https://www.jfklibrary.org/archives/other-resources/john-f-kennedy-speeches/nuclear-test-ban-treaty-19630726

36. https://www.presidency.ucsb.edu/documents/remarks-the-signing-the-nuclear-nonproliferation-treaty

37. Record of Conversations in the CPSU with N. Ceausescu and I.G. Maurer, 17-18 March 1967

38. Record of Conversations in the CPSU with N. Ceausescu and I.G. Maurer, 17-18 March 1967

39. https://disarmament.unoda.org/wmd/nuclear/npt/#:~:text=The%20 NPT%20is%20a%20landmark,the%20five%20nuclear%2Dweapon%20 States.

40. https://history.state.gov/milestones/1969-1976/salt

41. https://history.state.gov/milestones/1969-1976/salt

42. https://millercenter.org/the-presidency/presidential-speeches/may-20-1971-remarks-announcing-agreement-strategic-arms

43. https://www.presidency.ucsb.edu/documents/remarks-ceremony-marking-entry-into-force-the-treaty-the-limitation-anti-ballistic-missile

44. https://www.presidency.ucsb.edu/documents/remarks-ceremony-marking-entry-into-force-the-treaty-the-limitation-anti-ballistic-missile

45. Interim Agreement on certain measures with respect to the limitation of strategic offensive arms (with protocol). Signed at Moscow on 26 May 1972 Authentic texts: English and Russian. Registered by the United States of America on 2 August 1974.

46. https://www.armscontrol.org/act/2002-01/us-withdrawal-abm-treaty-president-bushs-remarks-and-us-diplomatic-notes
47. Department of State - Text of Diplomatic Notes to Russia, Belarus, Kazakhstan, and Ukraine, December 13, 2001
48. https://www.voanews.com/a/a-13-a-2001-12-13-12-putin-66405747/549270.html
49. Vladimir Putin, "Presidential Address to the Federal Assembly," March 1, 2018, at http://en.kremlin.ru/events/ president/news/56957
50. https://www.presidency.ucsb.edu/documents/vienna-summit-meeting-remarks-president-brezhnev-and-president-carter-signing-the-treaty
51. https://history.state.gov/milestones/1969-1976/salt
52. https://atomicarchive.com/resources/treaties/salt-II.html
53. https://history.state.gov/milestones/1969-1976/salt
54. https://missilethreat.csis.org/missile/ss-20-saber-rsd-10/
55. https://www.theguardian.com/commentisfree/2024/dec/27/the-guardian-view-on-arms-control-essential-to-prevent-the-total-devastation-of-nuclear-war
56. https://www.armscontrol.org/factsheets/intermediate-range-nuclear-forces-inf-treaty-glance
57. https://www.reaganlibrary.gov/archives/speech/remarks-signing-intermediate-range-nuclear-forces-treaty
58. Remarks on Signing the Intermediate-Range Nuclear Forces Treaty | Ronald Reagan - https://www.reaganlibrary.gov/archives/speech/remarks-signing-intermediate-range-nuclear-forces-treaty
59. https://www.reaganlibrary.gov/archives/speech/remarks-signing-intermediate-range-nuclear-forces-treaty
60. https://www.reaganlibrary.gov/archives/speech/remarks-signing-intermediate-range-nuclear-forces-treaty
61. https://www.reaganlibrary.gov/archives/speech/remarks-signing-intermediate-range-nuclear-forces-treaty
62. https://www.reaganlibrary.gov/archives/speech/remarks-signing-intermediate-range-nuclear-forces-treaty
63. https://www.en.kremlin.ru/events/president/transcripts/59863
64. https://en.kremlin.ru/events/president/news/59431
65. https://www.nato.int/cps/en/natohq/official_texts_161122.htm
66. https://2017-2021.state.gov/u-s-intent-to-withdraw-from-the-inf-treaty-february-2-2019/
67. https://trumpwhitehouse.archives.gov/briefings-statements/statement-president-regarding-intermediate-range-nuclear-forces-inf-treaty/
68. [1] https://en.kremlin.ru/events/president/news/59455/print
69. https://washington.mid.ru/en/press-centre/news/statement_by_the_president_of_russia_on_the_unilateral_withdrawal_of_the_united_states_from_the_trea/
70. https://nsarchive2.gwu.edu/NSAEBB/NSAEBB203/
71. Reykjavik File - Previously Secret U.S. and Soviet Documents on the 1986 Reagan-Gorbachev Summit-Document 5 – Gorbachev's instructions to Reykjavik prep group, October 4, 1986

72. Reykjavik File - Previously Secret U.S. and Soviet Documents on the 1986 Reagan-Gorbachev Summit-Document 13 – U.S. Memorandum of Conversation, 12 October 1986 (3rd Meeting)

73. https://nsarchive2.gwu.edu/NSAEBB/NSAEBB203/
74. Reykjavik File - Previously Secret U.S. and Soviet Documents on the 1986 Reagan-Gorbachev Summit-Document 16 – Russian Transcript of Final Session, 12 Oct 1986
75. https://nsarchive2.gwu.edu/NSAEBB/NSAEBB203/
76. Reykjavik File - Previously Secret U.S. and Soviet Documents on the 1986 Reagan-Gorbachev Summit-Document 4 – Memo to Reagan from Secretary George Shultz, October 2, 1986
77. Reykjavik File - Previously Secret U.S. and Soviet Documents on the 1986 Reagan-Gorbachev Summit-Document 19 – Gorbachev's reflections on the flight back to Moscow, 12 Oct 1986
78. Reykjavik File - Previously Secret U.S. and Soviet Documents on the 1986 Reagan-Gorbachev Summit-Document 25 – National Security Decision Directive 250, November 3, 1986
79. Reykjavik File - Previously Secret U.S. and Soviet Documents on the 1986 Reagan-Gorbachev Summit-Document 28 – Gorbachev's Politburo Conference, December 1, 1986
80. Soviet-United States Joint Statement on the Treaty on Strategic Offensive Arms | The American Presidency Project - https://www.presidency.ucsb.edu/documents/soviet-united-states-joint-statement-the-treaty-strategic-offensive-arms

81. https://www.presidency.ucsb.edu/documents/soviet-united-states-joint-statement-the-treaty-strategic-offensive-arms
82. https://www.presidency.ucsb.edu/documents/soviet-united-states-joint-statement-the-treaty-strategic-offensive-arms
83. https://www.presidency.ucsb.edu/documents/remarks-president-gorbachev-and-president-bush-the-signing-ceremony-for-the-strategic-arms
84. https://www.presidency.ucsb.edu/documents/remarks-president-gorbachev-and-president-bush-the-signing-ceremony-for-the-strategic-arms
85. The Legacy of START and Related U.S. Policies - https://2009-2017.state.gov/t/avc/rls/126119.htm
86. The Legacy of START and Related U.S. Policies - https://2009-2017.state.gov/t/avc/rls/126119.htm
87. The Legacy of START and Related U.S. Policies - https://2009-2017.state.gov/t/avc/rls/126119.htm
88. The Legacy of START and Related U.S. Policies - https://2009-2017.state.gov/t/avc/rls/126119.htm

89. A New START in Prague | whitehouse.gov -
https://obamawhitehouse.archives.gov/blog/2010/04/07/a-new-
start?utm_source

90. Soviet-United States Joint Statement on the Treaty on Strategic
Offensive Arms | The American Presidency Project -
https://www.presidency.ucsb.edu/documents/soviet-united-states-
joint-statement-the-treaty-strategic-offensive-arms?utm_source

91. The President's News Conference With President Boris Yeltsin of
Russia in Moscow | The American Presidency Project -
https://www.presidency.ucsb.edu/documents/the-presidents-news-
conference-with-president-boris-yeltsin-russia-moscow-1?utm_source

92. Strategic Arms Reduction Treaty II - Center for Arms Control and
Non-Proliferation - https://armscontrolcenter.org/strategic-arms-
reduction-treaty-ii/

93. Strategic Arms Reduction Treaty II - Center for Arms Control and
Non-Proliferation - https://armscontrolcenter.org/strategic-arms-
reduction-treaty-ii/

94. Russian President Vladimir Putin's response to the U.S. decision to
withdraw from the ABM treaty -
https://www.atomicarchive.com/resources/documents/missile-
defense/putin-abm-remarks.html?utm_source

95. Remarks by President Obama and President Medvedev of Russia at
New START Treaty Signing Ceremony and Press Conference |
whitehouse.gov - https://obamawhitehouse.archives.gov/the-press-
office/remarks-president-obama-and-president-medvedev-russia-new-
start-treaty-signing-cere

96. A New START in Prague | whitehouse.gov -
https://obamawhitehouse.archives.gov/blog/2010/04/07/a-new-
start?utm

97. The President in Prague | The White House -
https://obamawhitehouse.archives.gov/video/The-President-in-
Prague/#transcript

98. The President in Prague | The White House -
https://obamawhitehouse.archives.gov/video/The-President-in-
Prague/#transcript

99. Remarks by President Obama and President Medvedev of Russia at
New START Treaty Signing Ceremony and Press Conference |
whitehouse.gov - https://obamawhitehouse.archives.gov/the-press-
office/remarks-president-obama-and-president-medvedev-russia-new-
start-treaty-signing-cere

100. Remarks by President Obama and President Medvedev of Russia at
New START Treaty Signing Ceremony and Press Conference |
whitehouse.gov - https://obamawhitehouse.archives.gov/the-press-
office/remarks-president-obama-and-president-medvedev-russia-new-
start-treaty-signing-cere

101. New START Treaty - United States Department of State -
https://www.state.gov/new-start-treaty

102. New START Treaty - United States Department of State -
https://www.state.gov/new-start-treaty

103. 2022 - Report On The Reasons That Continued Implementation Of The New START Treaty is in The National Security Interest Of The United States - United States Department of State - https://www.state.gov/report-on-the-reasons-that-continued-implementation-of-the-new-start-treaty-is-in-the-national-security-interest-of-the-united-states/?utm

104. 2023 Report to Congress on Implementation of the New START Treaty - United States Department of State - https://www.state.gov/bureau-of-arms-control-deterrence-and-stability/releases/2024/01/2023-report-to-congress-on-implementation-of-the-new-start-treaty

105. New START Treaty Aggregate Numbers of Strategic Offensive Arms - United States Department of State - https://www.state.gov/new-start-treaty-aggregate-numbers-of-strategic-offensive-arms-5/?utm_

106. New START Treaty Aggregate Numbers of Strategic Offensive Arms - United States Department of State - https://www.state.gov/new-start-treaty-aggregate-numbers-of-strategic-offensive-arms-5/?utm

107. Current U.S. Missile Defense Programs at a Glance | Arms Control Association - https://www.armscontrol.org/factsheets/current-us-missile-defense-programs-glance

108. Current U.S. Missile Defense Programs at a Glance | Arms Control Association - https://www.armscontrol.org/factsheets/current-us-missile-defense-programs-glance

109. https://www.spaceforce.mil/About-Us/

110. en.kremlin.ru - https://en.kremlin.ru/events/president/news/70565

111. Putin says Russia suspending participation in New START treaty, last nuclear weapons pact with U.S. - CBS News - https://www.cbsnews.com/news/russia-putin-us-nuclear-weapons-treaty-new-start-suspending-articipation/#:~:text=Moscow%20%E2%80%94%20Russian%20Presi dent%20Vladimir%20Putin%20declared%20Tuesday,tensions%20with %20Washington%20over%20the%20fighting%20in%20Ukraine.

112. en.kremlin.ru - https://en.kremlin.ru/events/president/news/70565

113. Putin says Russia suspending participation in New START treaty, last nuclear weapons pact with U.S. - CBS News

114. Recommendations for Congressional Priorities on Nuclear Weapons & Arms Control Policy During the 119th Congress | Arms Control Association - https://www.armscontrol.org/Recommendations-for-Congressional-Priorities-2025?utm

115. New START at a Glance | Arms Control Association - https://www.armscontrol.org/factsheets/new-start-glance?utm

116. Open Skies Treaty - https://2009-2017.state.gov/t/avc/trty/102337.htm

117. Treaty on Open Skies - Federal Foreign Office - https://www.auswaertiges-amt.de/en/aussenpolitik/themen/218432-218432?utm

118. Open Skies: Transparency, Confidence-Building, and the End of the Cold War on JSTOR - https://www.jstor.org/stable/j.ctvqsdq9x

119. Open Skies Treaty - https://2009-017.state.gov/t/avc/trty/102337.htm

120. Open Skies Treaty - https://2009-017.state.gov/t/avc/trty/102337.htm
121. Open Skies Treaty - https://2009-017.state.gov/t/avc/trty/102337.htm
122. Open Skies Treaty - https://2009-017.state.gov/t/avc/trty/102337.htm
123. Open Skies Treaty - https://2009-017.state.gov/t/avc/trty/102337.htm
124. Open Skies Treaty - https://2009-017.state.gov/t/avc/trty/102337.htm
125. Open Skies Treaty - https://2009-017.state.gov/t/avc/trty/102337.htm
126. The Open Skies Treaty: Background and Issues | Congress.gov | Library of Congress - https://www.congress.gov/crs-product/IN10502
127. The Open Skies Treaty at a Glance | Arms Control Association - https://www.armscontrol.org/factsheets/openskies?utm
128. DOD Statement on Open Skies Treaty Withdrawal > U.S. Department of Defense > Release - https://www.defense.gov/News/Releases/Release/Article/2195239/dod-statement-on-open-skies-treaty-withdrawal/
129. DOD Statement on Open Skies Treaty Withdrawal > U.S. Department of Defense > Release - https://www.defense.gov/News/Releases/Release/Article/2195239/dod-statement-on-open-skies-treaty-withdrawal/
130. Putin signs law taking Russia out of Open Skies arms control treaty | Reuters - Putin signs law taking Russia out of Open Skies arms control treaty | Reuters

131. https://en.kremlin.ru/events/president/news/65870?utm
132. Jahresabrüstungsbericht 2020 - https://www.auswaertiges-amt.de/resource/blob/2457644/7a4fbb16352c3d2c3587fbc014ce6d4a/abrbericht2020-data.pdf
133. The Moscow Treaty - https://2009-2017.state.gov/t/avc/trty/127129.htm#4
134. November 13, 2001 - Joint Statement by President George W. Bush and President Vladimir V. Putin on a New Relationship Between the United States and Russia - https://2009-2017.state.gov/t/avc/trty/127129.htm#4

135. November 13, 2001 - Press Conference by President Bush and Russian President Vladimir Putin - The East Room - https://2009-2017.state.gov/t/avc/trty/127129.htm#4
136. President Putin, for his part, stated at the Russian Embassy in Washington, DC on November 13, 2001 - https://2009-2017.state.gov/t/avc/trty/127129.htm#4
137. President Putin, for his part, stated at the Russian Embassy in Washington on December 13, 2001 - https://2009-2017.state.gov/t/avc/trty/127129.htm#4
138. LETTER OF TRANSMITTAL by George W. Bush – Addressed to the White House - June 20, 2002 – to the Senate of the United States - https://2009-2017.state.gov/t/avc/trty/127129.htm#4
139. Speech of Russian Federation President V. V. Putin to Representatives of the American Public and U.S. Politicians, November 13, 2001, Russian Embassy in Washington – Department of State Archive

140. SORT – Article (1) -The Moscow Treaty - https://2009-2017.state.gov/t/avc/trty/127129.htm
141. SORT – Article II - The Moscow Treaty - https://2009-2017.state.gov/t/avc/trty/127129.htm
142. SORT – Article III - The Moscow Treaty - https://2009-2017.state.gov/t/avc/trty/127129.htm
143. SORT, Article IV, Sections 2–3 - The Moscow Treaty - https://2009-2017.state.gov/t/avc/trty/127129.htm

144. LETTER OF TRANSMITTAL – George W. Bush - June 20, 2002 - To the Senate of the United States - The Moscow Treaty - https://2009-2017.state.gov/t/avc/trty/127129.htm#4
145. 2006 Annual Report on Implementation of the Moscow Treaty - https://2009-2017.state.gov/t/avc/rls/rpt/108870.htm
146. 2007 Annual Report on Implementation of the Moscow Treaty - https://2009-2017.state.gov/t/avc/rls/rpt/88187.htm
147. 2008 Annual Report on Implementation of the Moscow Treaty - https://2009-2017.state.gov/t/avc/rls/rpt/104637.htm
148. 2009 Annual Report on Implementation of the Moscow Treaty - https://2009-2017.state.gov/t/avc/rls/rpt/127122.htm
149. 2010 Annual Report on Implementation of the Moscow Treaty - https://2009-2017.state.gov/t/avc/rls/rpt/141429.htm
150. 2011 Annual Report on Implementation of the Moscow Treaty - https://2009-2017.state.gov/t/avc/rls/rpt/164828.htm
151. 2010 Annual Report on Implementation of the Moscow Treaty - https://2009-2017.state.gov/t/avc/rls/rpt/141429.htm
152. 2011 Annual Report on Implementation of the Moscow Treaty - https://2009-2017.state.gov/t/avc/rls/rpt/164828.htm
153. 2011 Annual Report on Implementation of the Moscow Treaty - https://2009-2017.state.gov/t/avc/rls/rpt/164828.htm

www.ingramcontent.com/pod-product-compliance
Lightning Source LLC
Chambersburg PA
CBHW031121020426
42333CB00012B/172